Patterns for Daily Prayer

Susan Sayers

PATTERNS FOR DAILY PRAYER

Copyright © 2011 Susan Sayers
Original edition published in English under the title PATTERNS FOR
DAILY PRAYER by Kevin Mayhew Ltd, Buxhall, England.
This edition copyright © Fortress Press 2019

All rights reserved. Except for brief quotations in critical articles or
reviews, no part of this book may be reproduced in any manner without
prior written permission from the publisher. Email copyright@
augsburgfortress.org or write to Permissions, Fortress Press, PO Box
1209, Minneapolis, MN 55440-1209.

First published as *A Lifetime of Moments* in 1992 by Kevin Mayhew Ltd.

Cover image: Photo by S-S-S on iStock
Cover design: Lauren Williamson

Print ISBN: 978-1-5064-5938-7

Contents

Introduction	5
Taking Your Pulse	7
Warming Up	11
Feeling the Rhythm	13
Stretching Outward	16
Cycling and Recycling	18
Health Check	23
Prayer Pattern for a Week of Days	25
A Year of Days	51
Favorite Prayers	159

Introduction

This book is written for those who would like to be praying people but don't see how this is possible, considering all the other demands on their time. It is also written for those who already "say their prayers," but sense their need to get closer to God.

You will not find here a book of prayers ready-made. This is more of a spiritual coloring book—the outlines are drawn, and you are helped and encouraged to color them in whatever colors suit you best.

Taking Your Pulse

Any physical fitness program begins with an exercise to find out where you are at the moment, and what your particular needs are. From this starting point a program can be individually planned for you, which takes into consideration your circumstances, and your present state of fitness.

Committing yourself to praying is rather like embarking on a spiritual fitness course, which will eventually become such a healthy habit that your praying will be a natural, energizing part of your life, whatever your age, weight, or physical health.

No one would want to commit themselves to a physical fitness routine unless they could see some fairly substantial advantages to be gained from it. I suspect that many potential pray-ers never get started because they feel prayer is a sort of dutiful extra, rather than something that will really do them good.

So I'm going to tell you what you will gain from becoming prayerful:

YOU WILL BECOME BEAUTIFUL!
YOU WILL BECOME RICH!
YOU WILL BECOME HAPPY!

(Before you start checking that you are reading the right book, let me reassure you that this is indeed a book about prayer!) I am of course talking about spiritual beauty, spiritual riches, and spiritual happiness, all of which are side effects when we are at one with the God who made us and loves us. This kind of beauty, richness, and happiness is far better value than the usual sort, since it can't be stolen, it won't suddenly let you down, and it doesn't finish just because you get old and die.

With so much to gain from praying, how can you afford to put it off any longer? Any stiffness and aches you may experience in the process of growing spiritually fitter will be worthwhile, and, as in physical fitness, they will actually be a sign of your progress.

Let's begin with the first exercise straight away.

Exercise 1

As you live for the next twenty-four hours, notice any moments when you are able to be on your own, or when no demands are being made on you. For some of you there will not be many; for others the moments may stretch into hours. You may think you won't find any at all, but try it and see. There are no moments that don't count, so include all the times during the twenty-four hours.

Exercise 2

During the next few days, use the moments. Don't waste them on worrying about the future or the past, but consciously live them as the present moment, where you are alive and God is loving you. That's all. You don't need to use any words at all; just feel those two things—the "NOW" and God's love.

When you have been doing exercise 2 for several days, you are ready to start your Praying Plan. It is best to be very firm with yourself about this, as you would be for any really important secular life change. Use the chart and your new awareness of where your time goes, so that you can plan a definite time for praying each day—perhaps five to ten minutes. The earlier in the day you can manage, the better. You may find that you can slightly extend one of those "moment" slots in your day or night. You may need to juggle a few activities to create a small space for your praying. But this planning is in itself a prayer: through taking the trouble to do it, your actions are saying to God, "Lord, I'm still not really sure about all this, or even about you, but I really do want to get to know you more."

If you complete the chart in pencil, you can always change it later on if your circumstances change.

My Prayer Plan

Day	Main Time	Back-up Time
Sunday		
Monday		
Tuesday		
Wednesday		
Thursday		
Friday		
Saturday		

Warming Up

We always need to adjust ourselves to any activity, and praying is no different. We can't expect to come crashing into our prayer times, our minds loaded down with plans and memories, and be able to switch off immediately from all of that into some kind of a "holy" mood. I can imagine the Lord must shake his head in affectionate exasperation when he sees us doing this, because we make life so impossibly difficult for ourselves.

In fact, Jesus says to us, "Come to me—my yoke is easy and my burden is light." So begin by settling your body, and relaxing each muscle in turn until you are no longer all knotted up. Breathe in and out regularly and naturally, thinking of yourself as breathing in God's peace, and breathing out all your frustrations, and the day's concerns.

Some people find music very helpful; others find it easier to pray while walking along or standing outside. Some people pray best lying down in bed, some sitting, some kneeling. So long as you are able to relax and yet stay alert, the actual position you adopt is entirely up to you, and I am sure the Lord is not going to mind—people look on outward appearances, but the Lord looks on the heart.

If you find that even after this conscious relaxing, something on your mind is still nagging you, try these suggestions.

If it is something simple and practical (Did I turn the gas down? Have I set the alarm?), then go and check, put it right, and come straight back.

If it is something you need to remember, make a written note of it and put it to one side. (It is a good idea to have paper and pencil beside you in any case.)

If it is a deep worry, tell the Lord about it, and ask him to help you put it to one side.

There are bound to be noises and activities going on around you. Don't try to pretend they don't exist—our God is real and living, and he's used to the real world. So just acknowledge each distraction, and accept it as part of the scenery. Your inner stillness is not dependent on shutting yourself off from the world. In fact you may find those noises don't interrupt but emphasize the stillness as you spend time in God's company.

After your prayer time, you will feel refreshed and rested. That is one of God's gifts to you, one of his blessings. "Come to me all of you who are hardworking and over-burdened," he says, "And I will refresh you."

Feeling the Rhythm

It is still a comparatively short time since most humans lived off the land, felt the seasons in their bones, and were close to the natural rhythms of night and day, the patterns of weeks, and moon cycles, and the circle of a year's passing. There is still in many people a vague nostalgia for such a natural order, and a deep need for closeness with the pulse of the universe we inhabit. We are increasingly aware of how inextricably our survival is tied up with other species, and how delicate the balance of life is.

Through being habitually tuned in to the mind of the God who created and sustains our universe, prayerful people help to keep our world in balance, and that is a profoundly important task in this age. As our planet turns, there is an unbroken chain of praying people, turning toward the God of Love and absorbing his love for the good of the world. The words of John Ellerton's hymn express it beautifully:

> As o'er each continent and island
> the dawn leads on another day,
> the voice of prayer is never silent,
> nor dies the strain of praise away.

> The sun that bids us rest is waking
> our brethren 'neath the western sky
> and hour by hour fresh lips are making
> thy wondrous doings heard on high.

To be part of this endless chain of prayer is a tremendous privilege, and also a great comfort. You may have thought you were just on your own in familiar surroundings, struggling to be born in prayer; yet in reality you are joined and encouraged by a vast crowd of other praying people of all different shapes, colors, ages, and cultures, all of whom are your brothers and sisters, because we are bound together in Christ's love. Even as I write this book, I pray for you who are reading it, and as you read and use it, I hope that you will pray for me. And as the great tides of prayer wash over our world, we enable God's kingdom to be established.

So as to emphasize this sense of a pulsing world, full of natural rhythms and cycles, I have arranged the daily praying pattern as a week of days, linked with the different ages of creation. This means that your prayer focus will shift gradually throughout each week, so as to range over many areas in an ordered way. Without some kind of discipline we could end up forgetting some areas, and inadvertantly excluding them. During the first week that you use it you may not be aware of the pattern, but if you use it regularly, week by week, I hope you will start to feel the sense of being bound up with all God's creation, as he intended us to be.

When Jesus's disciples asked him to teach them how to pray, he gave them a prayer pattern to use. What could be a better way to pray than following the Lord's teaching? You will find that this is the pattern set out for you every day of the week—not as a set prayer to gabble off in "automatic pilot" mode, but as the outline for you to color in with the colors of your own life, and your personality. I have included suggestions and help to get you praying, but the actual praying you will find you are doing for yourself in your own "language." I feel this is important, because praying is your own relationship and conversation with the Lord, and it should be natural and personal.

May God bless you abundantly as you seek his face in your prayers and stillness.

Stretching Outward

As you get used to thinking and praying alongside other people in your daily prayer times, you will find that you are noticing more people who need to be prayed for. Whereas before, your reaction to someone's accident, or rocky marriage, illness, or practical need, may have been to feel sorry for them, now your heart will be turning that sympathy into prayer. Instead of worrying around and around in circles, you will find you are bringing your concerns to the positive help of the God who loves those involved and can work for great good in their lives.

This is how the two commandments always work: as soon as we begin to love God and expend time worshipping him, we shall find our love for one another growing. And it is a love that, springing directly from God's love, can bring healing and release people to live in joy.

Praying can keep you in touch with those from whom you are separated, either by distance or death. Praying can bring you close to those from whom you have drifted apart. Praying makes you personally involved with those who before were only statistics on the news. When we pray, God's love can pour out through us to bind up the broken hearted, rebuild shattered lives, and set people free. Your deepening relationship with the God of Love is enabling you to stretch out in love to all those you meet and hear about.

It is a good idea to keep a record of any particular prayer concerns. You want to pray for each person regularly, but to do so every day during your main prayer time would be impractical for most of us. I find it helps to spread these regular concerns (such as those in your family, and your "neighbors") over the space of a week, or a month, and make a separate list of specific needs and thanksgivings so that you can begin to see the effects of prayer.

If you write lightly in pencil, you can alter your lists as circumstances change. If possible, find out the names of those you hear about, and pray for them by name, imagining yourself standing or sitting beside them in God's presence.

Cycling and Recycling

Cycling is good for the health; recycling is good for the health of our planet. While you are praying the Lord's prayer regularly each day, each week, you have been cycling. The prayer pattern is like a wheel that enables you to travel forward along the Way, and the first Christians were known as followers of the Way.

Apart from the hour, the day, and the week, the other main natural circle that influences our lives is the year. Important occasions in life are always marked out for celebration or remembrance annually, and all around us in the cycle of seasons, things germinate, grow, flourish, fruit, die back, and are regenerated. And suddenly, we're another year older.

I think this yearly cycle has much to teach us about spiritual things, and it is good to cycle through the year's seasons with our spiritual eyes open to learn from it. So what follows in this book is a year of days, marked off in monthly sections. Each month explores spiritually what is happening in the natural world, and each day has a very short meditation for you to think about during that day.

I hope that in reading these few sentences each day, you will sense the way we are bound up with God's created order; in a way, all these things are also our brothers and sisters. All too often a frenetic, artificial order is imposed on our lives; moving in this way through the slow, rhythmic natural order can help us realign our priorities and feel in tune with the order God designed for his creation.

Prayer Concerns

Day	
Sunday	
Monday	
Tuesday	
Wednesday	
Thursday	
Friday	
Saturday	

To pray for monthly	
Week 1	Week 2
Week 3	Week 4

SPECIAL PRAYER NEEDS		
DATE	SITUATION	OUTCOME

Health Check

At intervals in any fitness program it is important to have a health check, and sort out anything that needs changing or putting right. Regular spiritual health checks are just as important. We need to take time each year to look hard at ourselves in the flashlight of God's love, particularly at the darker corners we usually prefer to ignore.

All kinds of scaly bits of selfishness grow on us that need regular melting away; lumps of resentment or unforgiveness can turn malignant or fester in us; cataracts of insensitivity can damage our spiritual eyesight. And all these things need treatment. Happily, we know personally the Good Physician—Jesus always maintained that he had come to heal the spiritually sick.

So that you remember your appointment each year, make it an occasion that is special to you, and arrange to spend time on that day in the light of God's love, assessing yourself in his eyes, and welcoming his advice about what needs changing or putting right. Look at the direction your life is taking; look at how your life measures up to God's requirement that we must love him, and love one another. Look at where our treasure really lies. The Spirit will guide you in all this, and show you truths about yourself that are important if you are to grow healthy and strong.

Many people find it helpful to talk over these things with a spiritual director; many use the sacrament of reconciliation; many work on their own. But all will be working in the presence and loving power of God who longs for us to come to him for healing, so that he can relieve us of the burdens we carry, lift the loads that weigh us down, and give us the freedom and joy of his complete forgiveness.

Prayer Pattern
for a Week of Days

Sunday
The first day of the week

> Our Father, who art in heaven,
> hallowed be thy name.

Say slowly, once or several times, "Then God commanded, Let there be light, and light appeared."

Now allow the God who created light to bathe you in his light. You don't have to do anything; be passive and let his light and warmth wash around you.

> O Lord of my life,
> everything I am
> and everything I have
> comes from you,
> the source of all being,
> and I worship you.

Take time to worship your Lord, in stillness and love, wrapped in his light and consciously part of his creation.

> *Take time to reflect in God's stillness.*

Think particularly of the Church and pray for all bishops, priests, and ministers, especially those in your own parish. Where possible, mention them by name.

> Thy kingdom come;
> thy will be done on earth
> as it is in heaven.

Think of all the different Christian groups who will be worshipping God today all over the world. Remember our Lord's desire for unity.

> Thy kingdom come;
> thy will be done on earth
> as it is in heaven.

Think of those who may be unable to join other Christians today through illness, frailty, family difficulties, or political danger.

> Thy kingdom come;
> thy will be done on earth
> as it is in heaven.

> *Take time to reflect in God's stillness.*

> Give us this day
> our daily bread.

Remember that spiritual feeding is as important to our life, health, and growth as physical feeding. Thank God for feeding you now. Pray that all who gather to worship today may be receptive to God's feeding.

> Give us this day
> our daily bread.

Pray for all who are hungry for meaning and value in their lives.

> Give us this day
> our daily bread.
>
> *Take time to reflect in God's stillness.*
>
> Forgive us our trespasses
> as we forgive those
> who trespass against us.

Bring to mind, however painfully, your habits that cause others or your own body distress.

Tell your Lord about them. Ask him to free you of them, and use even your weaknesses for his glory.

Bring to mind any who have hurt or insulted you in any way.

Can you forgive them?

Offer as much forgiveness as you honestly can at the moment, and ask God to help you forgive more completely.

> Lead us not into temptation
> but deliver us from evil.

Thank God for the light of his love that always surrounds you.

Ask him to keep you aware of this through the difficult times.

> For the kingdom, the power
> and the glory are yours
> forever and ever! Amen.

Now go in the light of Christ, and bring his light to all you meet.

Turn to today's date for the prayer.

Monday
The second day of the week

> Our Father, who art in heaven,
> hallowed be thy name.

Be still in the presence of the Lord.

"So God made a great vault and separated the water under it from the water over it . . . and the vault he called 'sky.'"

As the Lord of creation works to bring order out of chaos, trust him now with the ordering and "hallowing" of your life.

> Holy, holy, holy Lord,
> let all creation
> hold your name in reverence.

Take time to reflect in God's stillness.

Think of the important decisions you need to make in your life.

Ask the Lord of your life to direct you clearly, not your way but his.

> Thy kingdom come;
> thy will be done on earth
> as it is in heaven.

Think of any political decisions that are being made at the moment and important discussions where people hold strongly opposing views.

> Thy kingdom come;
> thy will be done on earth
> as it is in heaven.

Think of any areas where there is conflict and chaos. Ask the Lord of reconciliation and order to transform the situation.

> Thy kingdom come;
> thy will be done on earth
> as it is in heaven.
>
> *Take time to reflect in God's stillness.*
>
> Give us this day
> our daily bread.

Remember before God any practical needs you have that are worrying you. He who has made you cares about such things, and loves to hear you trusting him with them, whether these needs are financial, emotional, or organizational or long-term or acute. Take time to confide in him and ask for his help and advice.

> Give us this day
> our daily bread.
>
> *Take time to reflect in God's stillness.*

Much human disorder and chaos is caused by lack of forgiveness. Bring to the Lord any situations where forgiveness and acceptance are needed in the world, in your country, or in your neighborhood.

> Forgive us our trespasses
> as we forgive those
> who trespass against us.

In our own lives it's the same. Bring to the Lord any relationships you find difficult. In your imagination, stand beside this person in God's presence as you say with all your heart:

> Forgive us our trespasses
> as we forgive those
> who trespass against us.

Take time to reflect in God's stillness.

Think of any conversations or situations that are likely to be difficult today—at home, at work, while traveling.

> Lead us not into temptation
> but deliver us from evil.

Know that the God of order will be in control. Thank him for this.

> For the kingdom, the power,
> and the glory are yours
> forever and ever! Amen.

God is the same before the beginning, at this present moment, and for all time and eternity, and he loves you. So go in the peace of his everlasting presence and do not be afraid.

Turn to today's date for the prayer.

Tuesday
The third day of the week

Everything around you is held in being by God. Take time to become aware of this, breathing naturally and keeping your body in stillness.

"So the earth produced all kinds of plants, and God was pleased with what he saw." Feel yourself to be part of the richness of creation as you give him the glory:

> Our Father, who art in heaven,
> hallowed be thy name.
>
> *Say the words slowly, once or several times.*
>
> *Take time to reflect in God's stillness.*

Think of the planet we all share, particularly thanking God for the abundance of plant life and all grown food. Think of our need to look after it responsibly.

> Thy kingdom come;
> thy will be done on earth
> as it is in heaven.

Remember those living in areas of severe drought, where crops have failed, food is scarce, and clean water unheard of.

Think of those working to irrigate and improve living conditions.

> Thy kingdom come;
> thy will be done on earth
> as it is in heaven.

Be still in the presence of the Lord.

Think of the desperately poor and the starving. Stand alongside them and pray:

> Give us this day
> our daily bread.

Think of those who are over-nourished physically, but whose lives are desperately empty and starved of value. Stand alongside them and pray:

> Give us this day
> our daily bread.

Be still in the presence of the Lord.

Think now of any opportunities you have missed where you could have shown kindness, patience, love, or understanding.

Think particularly of the way you behave with those closest to you.

> Forgive us our trespasses
> as we forgive those
> who trespass against us.
>
> Lord of life and growth,
> help me to grow in your love
> so that I may bear good fruit.

Think of the inequalities of our world: the greed, complacency, and selfishness that damage our sharing. Recognize with humility that we are all partly to blame.

> Forgive us our trespasses
> as we forgive those
> who trespass against us.

> *Be still in the presence of the Lord.*

> Lead us not into temptation
> but deliver us from evil.

In our world, wheat often struggles to grow among many kinds of powerful weeds. It is not easy to stand up for what is right in a lazy and self-indulgent society.

> Lead us not into temptation
> but deliver us from evil.

Good fruiting plants can be choked by the cares and distractions of thorns; their growth is stunted, and their fruit is damaged.

> Lead us not into temptation
> but deliver us from evil.

Yet in all things, the Lord of life has the victory, and his love is stronger even than death. Give thanks with your whole self as you say:

> For the kingdom, the power,
> and the glory are yours
> forever and ever! Amen.

Stay rooted in Christ and bear fruit in abundance.

Turn to today's date for the prayer.

Wednesday
The fourth day of the week

"So God made the two larger lights, the sun to rule over the day and the moon to rule over the night; he also made the stars. And God was pleased with what he saw."

God is Lord of all our time and space. Spend some time now imagining the vastness of this universe. Think of yourself on this particular point of the planet—like a globe. Now think of yourself on earth within the solar system, and the system within our galaxy. Worship the creator of all this.

> Our Father, who art in heaven,
> hallowed be thy name.

Be still in the presence of the Lord.

Think of those whose time is spent in excessively hard labor; those under great pressure, and those who never have time to call their own. Name them now, bringing their lives into the beauty of God's timeless presence.

> Thy kingdom come;
> thy will be done on earth
> as it is in heaven.

Think of those for whom time drags past, those for whom each minute is filled with pain, and those who cannot sleep at night.

> Thy kingdom come;
> thy will be done on earth
> as it is in heaven.

Think of those whose hearts are heavy and fearful at the thought of starting another day; think of those for whom the night is terrifying.

> Thy kingdom come;
> thy will be done on earth
> as it is in heaven.
>
> *Be still in the presence of the Lord.*
>
> Give us this day
> our daily bread.

Day and night people are working to provide for our practical needs. Think of all the shift workers and all those working in farming and food production, industry and power, health and education, and cleaning and delivering. As you bring each group to mind, bring them also to God's care.

> Give us this day
> our daily bread.

Think of one or two people who do not know Jesus. Stand alongside them in your mutual need for the bread of life.

> Give us this day
> our daily bread.

Be still in the presence of the Lord.

Think of the way you spend your days and your nights. Ask your Lord to show you anything that needs changing, anything you are doing that works against his Way of Love.

> Forgive us our trespasses
> as we forgive those
> who trespass against us.

Ask him to give you both courage and opportunity to put things right.

Be still in the presence of the Lord.

> And lead us not into temptation
> but deliver from evil.

There is much that is evil, both around us in the world, and in us. But our God is Lord of our darkness as well as our light. In his loving power we shall be safe, no matter what evil we come across today. Put yourself and this day into his hands.

> And lead us not into temptation
> but deliver us from evil.

Be still in the presence of the Lord.

Remember once more that you exist as a precious part of the entire universe. The earth rolls through day and night, and as you are praising God, your spiritual voice is forming part of the unending music of praise.

> For the kingdom, the power,
> and the glory are yours
> forever and ever! Amen.

Go in the name of Christ, and bring his joy to the world.

Turn to today's date for the prayer.

Thursday
The fifth day of the week

"Let the water be filled with many kinds of living beings, and let the air be filled with birds."

When we empty ourselves of distraction and allow God space, he can fill us, too. Take time with your body quite still, breathing naturally. Think of breathing space into your life.

> Our Father, who art in heaven,
> hallowed be thy name.

As you acknowledge the holiness of God, allow him to fill you with his love.

> *Be still in the presence of the Lord.*

Think of some of the sea creatures and the birds, and thank God for them. Think of the planet we all share.

> Thy kingdom come;
> thy will be done on earth
> as it is in heaven.

Think of all the different areas of your life, and the people you meet in each area. Think of these as spaces that God can fill and use.

> Thy kingdom come;
> thy will be done on earth
> as it is in heaven.

Be still in the presence of the Lord.

Sea creatures and birds of the air remind us to live simply, without undue anxiety about food, clothing, and shelter.

> Give us this day
> our daily bread.

Look at the clothes you are wearing now; think of what you possess and thank God for it. Ask God to help you trust more in him and less in the security of your material possessions.

> Give us this day
> our daily bread.

Be still in the presence of the Lord.

Call to mind any times you have been envious of someone for what they possessed or achieved, any times you have acted, not so much as a steward of your possessions, time, and territory but more as a grudging and miserly owner of them.

> Forgive us our trespasses
> as we forgive those
> who trespass against us.

Call to mind any times when you have been possessive of other people and failed to respect their precious, God-given humanity. Stand beside them now.

> Forgive us our trespasses
> as we forgive those
> who trespass against us.

> *Be still in the presence of the Lord.*

We can never expect to like everyone we have contact with. After all, we are so different. But we are commanded to treat one another with love. Bring to the Lord any situations where this is hard.

> Lead us not into temptation
> but deliver us from evil.

So you need never rely on your own resources of strength! Give God all the glory for this.

> For the kingdom, the power,
> and the glory are yours
> forever and ever! Amen.

Go in the freedom of God's love, to love others to freedom.

Turn to today's date for the prayer.

Friday
The sixth day of the week

"Let the earth produce all kinds of animal life: domestic and wild, large and small—and it was done. Then God created human beings, making them to be like himself. He created them male and female."

God allows the earth to produce what is natural to it. In love there is always this freedom and potential. Spend time recognizing that your shape, your features, your characteristics are God's good idea, and he needs you to fulfill part of his wonderful plan. You are his child and he is your God.

> Our Father, who art in heaven,
> hallowed be thy name.

Be still in the presence of the Lord.

Remember that in God's kingdom there is unconditional caring, one for another. Think of those who are uncared for or despised. Stand beside them in God's presence.

> Thy kingdom come;
> thy will be done on earth
> as it is in heaven.

Remember how much God loves variety, color, and abundance. Think of the sadness caused by racial prejudice, and the social pressures on people to conform in order to be accepted.

> Thy kingdom come;
> thy will be done on earth
> as it is in heaven.
>
> *Be still in the presence of the Lord.*
>
> Give us this day
> our daily bread.

Recognize that, along with all creatures, we are dependent on God for everything. Offer all food preparation and eating as times to work in partnership with our Lord. Pray for those who have grown and prepared your food today.

> Give us this day
> our daily bread.
>
> *Be still in the presence of the Lord.*
>
> Forgive us our trespasses
> as we forgive those
> who trespass against us.

God was pleased to see the creatures he had made. Call to mind the selfishness and pride that make you critical or resentful of others. Think too, of those who have been critical or resentful of you.

> Forgive us our trespasses
> as we forgive those
> who trespass against us.

Think of those rejected and despised, those imprisoned and unjustly treated. As a member of the human race, plead for mercy.

> Forgive us our trespasses
> as we forgive those
> who trespass against us.

Think of the potential beauty of a world created in love; call to mind our destructiveness and lack of peace.

> Forgive us our trespasses
> as we forgive those
> who trespass against us.

> *Be still in the presence of the Lord.*

We have the capacity for great good. Or we are free to choose evil. Only in the all-powerful God shall we be able to resist temptation.

> Lead us not into temptation
> but deliver us from evil.

God's power and love are always sufficient for us. It is his good pleasure to give us the kingdom. Enjoy this encouragement and truth in his company.

> For the kingdom, the power,
> and the glory are yours
> forever and ever! Amen.

In Jesus's name, live life abundantly.

Turn to today's date for the prayer.

Saturday
The seventh day of the week

And so the whole universe was completed. By the seventh day God had finished what he had been doing and stopped working. He blessed the seventh day.

You have completed another week of your life. In stillness, bring to the Lord of creation what you have tried to do, what has been achieved, and what has failed. All of it is precious. Remember by name any of God's other children who particularly need your prayer. Feel at one with them and all God's children in the presence of the father who loves you.

> Our Father, who art in heaven,
> hallowed be thy name.

Allow your Lord to fill your body, your mind, and your spirit with his peace. It is the peace of knowing that eternal good is accomplished, the peace of a created being at one with the creator.

Be still in the presence of the Lord.

> Thy kingdom come;
> thy will be done on earth
> as it is in heaven.

Who else has the words of eternal life? No one. As you sense the perfect joy and beauty of God's peace, long for his kingdom to be established and his will, not ours, to be done.

> Thy kingdom come;
> thy will be done on earth
> as it is in heaven.

Think of the areas and situations in our world that desperately need the love our God offers. Think of the people who need his healing, liberating love.

> Thy kingdom come;
> thy will be done on earth
> as it is in heaven.

Think of the people who are living the kingdom and acting as vital channels of God's peace and love. Rejoice with them and share their hope and delight.

> Thy kingdom come;
> thy will be done on earth
> as it is in heaven.

> *Be still in the presence of the Lord.*

> Give us this day
> our daily bread.

We all need times of rest, relaxation, and refreshment. On this seventh day, allow God to refresh and revitalize you. Ask him to help you put things in perspective and realign your priorities.

> Give us this day,
> our daily bread.//
>
> *Be still in the presence of the Lord.*
>
> Forgive us our trespasses
> as we forgive those
> who trespass against us.

Think of the word "trespass" as meaning encroaching on others' territory, or invading their privacy. Recall with sorrow the times when you have been demanding, irritating, or provocative. Recall the times you have been used, neglected, or misunderstood. (You must recall in order to forgive.)

> Forgive us our trespasses
> as we forgive those
> who trespass against us.
>
> *Be still in the presence of the Lord.*

Jesus is the Way. Allow him to lead you through each second of your life.

> Lead us not into temptation
> but deliver us from evil.

You have been made by the God of Love; his love continues to make you a new creation. It is his doing, not yours. Accept this and relinquish another layer of self.

> For the kingdom, the power,
> and the glory are yours
> forever and ever! Amen.

Go out with joy and be led forth with peace.

Turn to today's date for the prayer.

A Year of Days

January

1 We spend so much of our time looking back over what has already happened, and forward to plan what will happen in the future. Often the present moment flies past without us noticing. Yet the stillness of the present is the closest we can get to understanding eternity, which is a constant "now."

2 When you become aware of the present moment, it has the effect of bringing space into your life, however busy and rushed your schedule. It relaxes and refreshes. It helps you notice and appreciate things you have gotten used to ignoring or taking for granted. And you can do it anywhere at any time. Try it today while you are waiting for something or somebody. Just remind yourself that this is "now."

3 You are here now because God chose to create you. He loves you the way you are and understands everything that makes you act and react the way you do. In some ways he knows you better than you know yourself, and he delights in you with the affection of a loving parent for a precious child.

4   You are unique. No one anywhere has exactly your soup of genes; no look-alike is exactly like you in temperament and character. Such individuality helps us realize the personal nature of the God we worship.

5   When you value yourself and other people as the unique and precious result of a creative, loving God, you will find you are treating yourself and others with a new respect and reverence. If God considers us worth making and looking after, then we are all important enough to be listened to, included, thoughtfully treated, and helped regardless of our age, appearance, or earning potential.

6   The wise men traveled through darkness to discover the Light of the world. Where you are going may be dark, and the ground uneven. Don't expect to see the whole route at once—that will come later. For now, be content that God will show you where you are treading and where the next immediate step is to be.

7   "Don't be afraid," says the Lord. "Remember that you are my own child, and I see your faithfulness. I know and understand your difficulties. Lean on me—trust me with your whole weight. I am supporting you, and I shall always support you, so you need not be afraid."

8. Soil needs to be broken up and left for the frost and wet to work on over the winter. Although nothing much is actually growing at the moment, the weather is working on the soil to prepare it for growth later on. Some periods of our life are like this. In themselves they seem empty and desolate, frozen and unproductive. It may be that ground is being prepared for rich growth later on.

9. Suffering and grief are bare, raw, windswept landscapes. Yet it is often in the earth of our suffering that seeds of compassion are sown. At the time everything may look hopeless and bleak, and it will not help us much to pretend otherwise. But praising the God of creation at such times is the most precious offering we can give, and it will help us to face the wasteland of our lives, knowing that even here God is in control; this experience may well be turning you into rich, fertile soil.

10. Many of the trees are shut down at this time of year and production is at a standstill. Yet the trees are not dead—we know they will be sprouting new buds in a month or two. If you find yourself feeling envious, it could be that your life is simply too busy and rushed for your health. It is not being lazy to cater to the body and spirit's need for rest and relaxation for some time each day. Even if you can only manage a couple of minutes, shut down production and activity completely and allow yourself space to be refreshed and revitalized.

11. You may wonder some days, how there will ever be enough time for you to do all that needs to be done. Panic can easily set in, so can muscle tension and irritability. You will easily recognize your own particular warning signs. Take a deep breath, hold it, and then slowly release it. Ask God to show you what the priorities are. Remember, he will be giving you your time quite slowly—second by second, and only one moment at a time! So live and work in each moment, doing whatever is most important for that particular time. You will find that although you may not fit in everything YOU planned to get done, you will have plenty of time to do all that is necessary.

12 Just as we need space ourselves, we need to accept enforced space. Even if we are not making much progress toward the counter in a shop or bank even if the traffic is horrendous and we are only moving at two miles in two weeks, still we are moving steadily toward life after death. Still we are moving steadily through time toward eternity.

13 Learn to relinquish the idea that we have a right to total control of time. There are bound to be occasions when our best laid plans fail, and we so often end up fuming when this happens. Instead, welcome these times as reminders that we are stewards, and not owners. Offer the enforced waiting for God to use, and yes, even thank him that your disrupted day has given you the opportunity to be flexible.

14 We must also allow space in our relationships. Love can sometimes turn into possessiveness. We long for the best for those we love, but we assume that they should agree with us about what "best" is. We all need to check that we are not in fact trying to impose our will on others, for this is not love but domination.

15 Earth takes time to be prepared, and many seeds require a time of wintering before germination is possible. Be content for some things to take time, and do not rush them. This is particularly true in marriage relationships, where we are often pressured by society, and can so easily grow "greenhouse" relationships that are forced, vigorous, but quickly die. We need to allow our relationships space to grow, and sometimes, just space to be.

16 Humility is being earth-like. We tread earth underfoot; it is often known as "soil" or "dirt," yet it is also our security—our "ground," from which all life grows. It is, above all, an enabler, just as we can be when we hold ourselves available to be used.

17 We shall not be available for God to use unless we keep ourselves clear of stones and weeds, and allow ourselves to be worked on. Think of some of the worst things that have happened to you and thank God for the privilege of living through such hardship and distress. He can then redeem those times, and give you back "the years that the locusts have eaten." Your acceptance makes this impossibility possible.

18 We may know lots of information about someone, but we can't begin to really know them until we spend time in their company, talking, listening, working, and relaxing together. It is just the same with Jesus. Don't be content with knowing about him today — get to know him personally by spending time in his company.

19 Today has never yet been lived, and God has decided that you will be one of those living it. Be alert, then — you are the only person he can use for a particular task today. That's how important you are.

20 What you may consider your weakest moments may in fact be the times when you are most in cooperation with God and least likely to thwart his plans by meddling with your own self-importance.

21 Keep in mind the knowledge that God considers you one of his good ideas, and rejoices in your existence. He chose that you should exist, and he will never give up on you or abandon you.

22 The deeper the relationship between you and the loving God who made you, the more fulfilled you will be, since you will become increasingly like you were made to be—the perfect person to be living your life with your relationships in the particular area of time and space that you fill.

23 If you have been praying for God to rescue you, you need to recognize the boat he sends; things may not happen in quite the way you expect.

24 When God answers our prayers he has in mind the greatest good for all his people and all creation. At the time, if we have already planned a cozy little answer, we may find it frustrating that he doesn't always take us up on our brilliant ideas. But later, on looking back, we may well be able to see how much more far-reaching and valuable was God's version of timings and events.

25 Unless we have had the privilege of suffering we shall be unable to respond to suffering in others. So when you next find yourself frail, vulnerable, or suffering, don't resent it and thereby discard its benefits; greet it as the raw material for great blessing.

26 When we approach God and ask him to make himself known to us, it is not like shopping, or a banking transaction. God is no dutiful puppet of our whims and wishes, to be summoned like a genie whenever we rub the lamp using a particular set of words. How dare we treat the Lord of heaven with such arrogance! Come before him in humility; wait for him with love. And when you feel the joyful reality of his presence, you will realize that he has been there all along, in ways you never suspected.

27 Like clay that is dug out of the ground, we can be worked, by God, the potter, into bowls and pots of various different sizes and for different purposes. Don't shout out instructions to the master potter, "lump of clay"! He knows exactly what shape you need to be for what your particular work is. And a flower pot would make a pretty useless cream jug. Trust the potter, "lump of clay"!

28 Sandy soil drinks up water readily, but it drains away fast. Clay soil is so set in one hard mass that the water can't even get in until it has softened up a bit. Overworked soil has been so busy growing things for years without a break that it needs a good rest and some input before it can be used again.

29 If you tend to be sandy soil, try disciplining yourself by scheduling regular, daily prayer into your life as a priority. If you tend to be like clay, unwilling to accept change and usually resisting new and different ideas, try getting yourself used to being flexible by varying your daily and weekly routine, and doing something out of the ordinary at least once a week.

30 Check that your life is not unrealistically full. If you find you are deeply weary, look at areas in your life that could be simplified. It is easy for Christians to become so involved in good works of various kinds that none of the good works get properly done. Beware: overwork can lead to resentment, a critical spirit and neglect of those closest to you.

31 Remember that physically you are dust, and will eventually return to dust. That isn't as depressing as it sounds! Remember it whenever material things are getting you down, or becoming so important to you that you are worrying about them. Compared with eternal life, our physical time here is really quite short, so all those "things"— even your aging appearance—are a lot less important than they seem.

February

1. Roots, hidden from view, grow down into the earth before any green shoots appear on the surface. So it is with our growth in Christ. We can't expect any green shoots, let alone any fruit, unless we have a strong, hidden root system.

2. Roots absorb water and nourishment so that the plant can grow. Are you rooted near the stream of living water that will never dry up, or are some of your roots relying on puddles of water that could dry up at any time?

3. One way to test out your roots is to notice how you react when one of the "puddles" you rely on lets you down. This may be a person, a possession, an ambition, a routine, or an expectation. The more deeply you are upset, the more reliance you must have been placing on this particular "puddle."

4. Put your trust in the only totally reliable and faithful One. Let yourself be deeply rooted by the stream where living water flows.

5   Strong roots anchor us securely so that when storms come we can stand firm. The Lord never promises his children an easy life, or immunity from such storms. When they blow, we shall find them just as powerful as everyone else. The difference is that in God we are ultimately safe, and in his strength no storm, however powerful, is able to overcome us. Nothing—absolutely nothing—can ever separate us from the love of God that is in Christ Jesus.

6   How can we develop a strong root system that will nourish us and help us stand firm? Jesus advises us to watch and to pray. To be effective, then, our watchfulness and prayerfulness need to be constant—second nature to us, and as natural as breathing and eating regularly.

7   You can't achieve constant prayerfulness in a day—more like a lifetime. So don't feel you must rush the process. Nor does it matter if you are starting out yet again after many lapses. The important thing is to begin— every day is a beginning.

8 Start with a very little time set apart for prayer, you can really keep to regularly. It may help to keep something that reminds you to pray, in a place you go to regularly — like a mirror in the bathroom, for instance, or by the coffee maker in the kitchen. Whenever you catch sight of your memory jogger, lift your heart in thankfulness to God; your roots are beginning to grow.

9 Love prompts us to pray. Whenever you find yourself serving others in a practical way, however simple, let the act become a prayer by recognizing God's presence in it.

10 Our society encourages us to be self-indulgent. That is never the way of Christ. But if we are going to be self-disciplined, we need to do it without becoming self-righteous or critical of others. Keep the root growth well hidden from people's view and from any praise there may be.

11 You have been born with certain physical characteristics that have come down to you through your ancestors; however much you may dislike some of these, each can be used in some way for God's glory — provided you admit they exist, and offer them.

12 You have been born with certain gifts and talents. Before you jump in to disagree, please forget the world's idea that a talent is only worthwhile if it's better than anyone else's. In God's vocabulary a gift or talent is anything you do well, even if millions of others also do it well. Now, we have established that you have certain gifts and talents—do you pray about how they can best be used?

13 Sometimes we are haunted by things that have happened to us, or things we regret doing, way back in our past. Unfortunately, the more we try to bury them, the more they fester and hurt us, damaging the present. God is Lord of all time and all situations—he longs to rid you of these "ghosts." Let him work his healing in you.

14 You may have seen plants that are pot-bound. The roots are cramped and twisted around and around themselves, craving more space and more nourishment. We are sometimes like that. We try to grow in prayer as mature Christians while still trapped in a child-sized pot. We need to be re-potted!

15 If you are feeling root-bound in your prayer, take a trip to your church library or local Christian bookshop and start reading to extend your knowledge of the faith, deepen your understanding, and challenge yourself to fresh insights once again. Give those roots of yours a chance to stretch!

16 Roots need the word of God for nourishment; not just a quick glance at a Sunday Bible passage, but daily prayerful study of this most rich and valuable library. If you wait to start until you have time, you will probably never get going. If you begin today, you will soon be wondering why you didn't start sooner.

17 Roots need to reach out to God in worship and praise. It is so easy for our prayer to slump into a catalog of needs. Yet the thankfulness and praise is an outpouring of love, and we need this. It is only through giving ourselves to God in worship that we shall grow more and more like him, our faces shining as they reflect his glory.

18 Another fundamental spiritual need is fellowship in worship. Christianity is a very social religion—the Church Christ founded is a community, and we are to encourage one another in the faith. Don't try to go it alone; you need other Christians, and they need you.

19 Gardeners and farmers know all too well that roots can get attacked. At first the plant may continue looking good, but eventually the root problem begins to show in the leaves and fruit. You may be quite a mature tree spiritually, but if your hidden root growth starts to go wrong, sooner or later it will show in your life.

20 Sin is invasive and subtle; if we allow some wrong thought or action to occupy us, we will quickly find we are getting used to it being there, and will no longer recognize it as sin.

21 Don't confuse temptation with sin; but deal with temptation quickly, before it can ripen to sin.

22 Healthy roots are far less likely to succumb to parasites. Christians who are spiritually well-nourished and well-rooted, are less likely to succumb to sin. But that certainly doesn't mean they are less likely to be attacked.

23 Roots can hold together the topsoil and prevent erosion. Our world desperately needs people with the strong roots of hidden spiritual growth. Each praying person is helping to protect the world from spiritual and moral erosion. Each new praying person is helping to reclaim the wasteland.

24 If there are any impossibly hard and rocky situations in your life, remember that quiet, strong roots have the power in their growing to split rocks apart.

25 Roots persist in their growing all the time the plant is growing. We never lose the need for concentrating on this deep, secret part of our spiritual life.

26 While the roots remain alive, even a tree stump can sprout again. It was from the root, or stump, of Jesse that the Messiah was to come. So whatever goes disastrously wrong in our lives, and however much we fail, it is our roots in Christ that enable us to be patient in suffering, and have peace and hope.

27 May the Lord of all faithfulness keep you faithful in all things, and give you the courage to persevere.

28 The Lord has promised that if you are rooted near his life-giving water, you will be richly blessed. And your reliable fruit and shade will enable you to bless others.

29 Your roots determine your life; stay rooted in nothing less than the source of love.

March

1 As you become more rooted in prayer, you will actually find your life changing. This should really come as no surprise, since you are increasingly open to the immensely powerful God; yet it often does happen unexpectedly and it is helpful to be prepared—never let Jesus into your heart, unless you are prepared for change!

2 Like dogs rolling in the dust after they've been bathed, most of us are comfortable with our own spiritual scruffiness, and don't welcome the thought of fundamental changes. Yet as our prayer life deepens, we may find ourselves becoming dissatisfied and uncomfortable with some areas of ourselves. This sense of discomfort is unsettling, and we may at first interpret it in a negative way. In fact it is a positive sign of progress, so welcome it.

3   As we allow God's Spirit more access to our lives, the light of God will begin showing the accumulated debris and dust that, in the gloom, had gone unnoticed. That is why the sense of discontent is progress—it shows that God's Spirit within us is beginning to lead us into all truth by gently revealing to us what needs to be changed or discarded in our lives.

4   Follow the lead of God's Spirit within you; become willing to change what needs changing.

5   As your prayer life deepens you will find that God is gradually taking your heart of stone and giving you a heart of flesh—he is making you a new creation.

6   The Lord we worship is certainly a God of power, but he is also full of gentleness and courtesy. He will never reveal to you more truth about yourself than you can cope with at the moment. So you can trust him with your spiritual growth and follow his promptings with confidence.

7   You may find your perspectives changing. Living prayerfully means that you are increasingly living both in this lifetime, and also in the context of eternity. Some things will begin to matter more, some will begin to lose their importance. This is spiritual regeneration—the freshness of new growth—and it may cause jarring in your lifestyle.

8   If this jarring in your lifestyle is not what you bargained for when you started praying more deeply, it may help to read over Jesus's conditions for being counted among his followers. It's in Matthew 16:24–25.

9   Just before a seed or bulb breaks out into new growth, considerable pressure builds up inside. In fact, it is this very pressure that breaks the hard outer shell and allows the new shoot to stretch outward and upward to the light. It is the same with us: we cannot grow up freely to new life without the old seed-casing splitting. Unless a grain of wheat "dies" it cannot yield a harvest.

10. As you become more deeply rooted in Christ through prayer, you will find yourself becoming concerned about situations in the world that had not bothered you before. Sometimes people find themselves actually moved to tears over the pain and sorrows of those who suffer, and thrilled by acts of love and kindness previously taken for granted.

11. Part of being rooted in God is the process of growing in God's love, and that means feeling things more sharply. Perhaps you remember what it felt like when you first fell in love; well, that freshness and intensity of vision is one of the side effects of a deepening love for God growing within you.

12. We sometimes think of falling in love as all that rosy glow surrounding a fresh and exciting relationship. There is, of course, another side to it; as soon as we fall in love we become much more vulnerable and can be badly hurt far more easily. This also happens when our love for God increases. And this is why we feel, hand in hand with a newfound joy, a new sensitivity to all the suffering and injustice of our world.

13 Since God loves each of us so deeply, he suffers with each of us in our various pockets of misery and pain, and as we become increasingly like him, we are bound to begin to feel that sense of suffering with others out of our greater love for them. Let it urge us to act more caringly.

14 We tend to pray fervently for those we deeply love. It follows, too, that our love toward those we pray for increases at remarkable speed. All kinds of difficult relationships have been smoothed out and redeemed by this amazing power. All kinds of impossible situations have been transformed through people praying fervently for them and in them.

15 We tend to remember the people we pray for, too. Get into the habit of committing those you meet and work with to the love and protection of the all-loving God.

16 As you pray, the channels are cleared for God to flow into you and through you. So characteristics of the loving Lord will begin to show in your own life. They may not be that obvious to everyone at first, but you will experience particular instances when you find yourself thinking or acting in an uncharacteristically loving way! This is the Lord of Love living within you, so enjoy giving him all the praise and glory.

17 We shall find that we are enabled to forgive others more readily and more completely. This capacity for forgiveness is a gift from God, and he may nudge us into using it by bringing to mind certain hurts and grievances we may have buried for years without really tackling. So be prepared.

18 If you find past hurts and grievances suddenly coming to mind, don't try to bury them all over again—this is a new God-given opportunity for you to lay the whole situation before the Lord and have it healed completely, once and for all.

19 Another mark of spiritual growth is a surprising new enthusiasm for learning more about God. You may find yourself actually seeking out quiet times for prayer, opening the Bible and reading it "thirstily," wanting to talk about the faith with other Christians. You are not turning into a freak; God is drawing you closer into the joy and freedom of living in his love.

20 It is important to recognize that new growth and deepening faith happen regularly to Christians at all stages of their journey; if we once feel we have attained full height, that is a sure sign that we are barely started in the growth God has in mind for us.

21 What if we can remember times of rapid growth but feel at a standstill at the moment? One thing is certain: we can never force even an inch of growth on our own, so relax. Allow the Lord to nourish you, and make a conscious effort to seek his face. Through God's love for you, and through your faithfulness, much hidden growth will be going on. Stronger root growth will eventually result in a flourishing tree.

22 Try not to rely on feelings alone. If you sit in one position for too long, you can no longer feel your feet. But you are not tempted to think they are not there. In the same way, there are times when we feel God's loving presence very strongly. There are other times when we may feel nothing, but that does not mean he is not there.

23 Darkness can sometimes encourage new shoots in plants. Think of the buckets we place over young rhubarb! Sometimes we may find that just when we are growing vigorously, we are plunged into spiritual darkness, which is not related to our own erected barriers. It may be that God is encouraging our faith to grow strongly during these times as our need for his light drives us to wait on him with longing.

24 Our new shoots are tender. At this point of growth they can so easily be crushed or discouraged. The powers of evil hate new growth intensely and will try to stamp it out before it gets stronger. So do not be surprised or discouraged if you now find yourself attacked for what you know is born of deeper prayer. It is only a sure sign that you are indeed growing.

25 Remember that you are not the only one growing fresh shoots of new life, and as you know for yourself, fresh shoots are tender. So be encouraging and careful in the way you respond to other Christians, so that you don't damage or stunt their tender growth in any way.

26 When in doubt about how to respond to anyone or anything, think down to those roots of yours—rush back to the Lord of Love and sit at his feet. It is he who has the words of eternal life, and his grace is sufficient for all your needs.

27 It is quite possible to encourage growth in one another, and we need to do this. Yet there are many times when we avoid talking about our faith, even when opportunities for doing so are presented. Get into the habit of being prayerfully "available" so that when such opportunities come up, you can recognize them and use them.

28 New shoots need light. The darkness of earth, which is essential for roots, does not provide ideal growing conditions for the fresh green shoots—in fact it can be disastrous to them. Seek out the fellowship of Christians so you can worship together and encourage one another.

29 Bring your prayerfulness into all the ordinary, everyday situations of living. Pray as you walk around the supermarket or wait at the checkout. Pray before a meeting with someone, on entering someone's home or place of work, as you prepare food or clean the bathroom. Your prayer life is not just for you, but for the world.

30 Shoots can sometimes begin with such enthusiasm that they start to run wild and straggly. They may need pruning to make their growth stronger and more effective. So be prepared to be pruned!

31 Pruning may hurt at the time; it may feel as if you have been cut off from what you were best at, and that can be very confusing. Be patient—the Lord is an expert gardener, and knows exactly how you will best develop and grow. If you are feeling severely pruned, be thankful that you are considered worth pruning!

April

1. For growth in our spiritual life to be maintained, feeding is essential. Yet there are many Christians who put themselves on dangerous spiritual diets much of the time. During this month we will be feeding each day on the word of God. Feeding involves taking in the word, chewing it over, and allowing it to become part of us. And we can never do this by glancing over it and then forgetting it, any more than we become physically satisfied from glancing at a slice of bread.

2. "The Lord is my shepherd; I shall want for nothing." *Psalm 23*
Repeat this until you have it by heart. You might find it helps to write it out and put it in your wallet or somewhere you refer to often throughout the day. Think about it, imagine it; think of yourself as one of the sheep or lambs. Know that God cares, and looks after you constantly.

3. "I love you, O Lord, my strength." *Psalm 18*
Our own love is fed by expressing our love for God. Say it at least once an hour throughout the day, preferably every five minutes. No, that isn't excessive! If you do it, you will find your love for God is like a pulse beating effectively in your life.

4. "Hide me in the shadow of your wings." *Psalm 17*

   As you chew on this through the day, you will find you are noticing God's presence in the ordinary and the unexpected. Feed on the truth that wherever you are and whatever you are doing, you are in reach of the almighty God of Love.

5. "The Lord lives!" *Psalm 18*

   When you feed on this amazing truth you will find comfort during hardship, encouragement during despondency, joy when things go wrong, and lightness of heart—even laughter—when you are getting bogged down in life's complications.

6. "The earth is the Lord's and everything in it." *Psalm 24*

   As you feed on this, your own attitudes to people and possessions and situations will be made new—renewed in keeping with the character of God himself.

7. "God reigns over the nations." *Psalm 47*

   Think on this whenever you see the news. It becomes both a longing for the coming of God's kingdom, and a reassurance that ultimately all is well and God has the victory over evil.

8 "Our God is a God who saves." *Psalm 68*
This Word, in all its simplicity, encompasses the glorious Good News of our faith. As you think over it, allow it to fill you with confident hope and joy.

9 "Unless the Lord builds the house, the work of the builders is useless." *Psalm 127*
A sobering thought to feed us today, but one we ignore at our peril. How often we plan and build in our lives without more than a passing reference to the Lord of all. Let this Word speak to any such projects in your own situation, where the Lord himself should be doing the building.

10 "The Lord is gracious and compassionate, slow to anger and rich in love." *Psalm 145*
Think over the implications of each of these qualities. What do they teach you about how you should be reacting to difficult situations? Allow the Lord to teach you his ways through feeding you with this, his word.

11 "The Lord is near to all who call on him." *Psalm 145*
This is not wishful thinking but a statement of fact we can rely on. Whenever you call on him you can be completely certain that he is closer to you than you are to yourself. And that is a profoundly liberating piece of knowledge.

12 "Let everything that has breath praise the Lord!" *Psalm 150*

Let your mind and imagination wander through the huge variety of living creatures this includes. Whatever else Christianity is, it is certainly never an exclusive club. Nothing could be more far-reaching or inclusive.

13 "You, O Lord, keep my lamp burning; my God turns my darkness into light." *Psalm 18*

It is worth taking the trouble to learn these words of truth by heart. There is no darkness at all that is beyond the reach of God's light; no situation too terrible for him to transform and redeem.

14 "I have hidden your word in my heart that I might not sin against you." *Psalm 119*

This is real feeding, when our spiritual nourishment becomes part of what we are and affects the way we think and feel. We are not asked to become a theological encyclopedia; we could do that and still remain separate from God's law of love. Instead we are asked to "take his word to heart" where it will change and renew us.

15 "When my spirit grows faint within me, it is you who know my way." *Psalm 142*

You do not have to be full of energy and health to be close to our God. There are times when we feel we are too weak or exhausted to pray. But that is to misunderstand praying. At such times of weakness, the Lord is very close, full of understanding and comfort. Our prayer may not be doing or saying anything—just resting in his love.

16 "The Lord rescued me because he delighted in me." *Psalm 18*

Whenever you find yourself doubting your value as a person, remember these words that proclaim a remarkable truth—the Lord delights in you. He knows everything about you and still he delights in you!

17 "The Lord will watch over your coming and going both now and forevermore." *Psalm 121*

While we are busily going about our lives, perhaps forgetful of God, we are never forgotten by him. Whatever we are doing and wherever we are, he is watching over us because he loves us.

18 "Great peace have they who love your law." *Psalm 119*

We all have a deep need for inner peace—peace of heart and mind. The advertising world recognizes this and plays on it. We are bombarded with suggestions as to how we can achieve this satisfying peace, and most involve buying various possessions. God's peace is different. First, it's free. Second, it really satisfies.

19 "My heart and my flesh cry out for the living God." *Psalm 84*

Our longing for God is one of his gifts, which can draw us closer to him.

20 "Turn to me and you will be saved, all you ends of the earth, for I am God, and there is no other." *Isaiah 45*

There is complete authority in these words, which we can trust because our God has shown himself to be utterly faithful. This is a firm promise—a promise that can set our lives free.

21 "Though the mountains may fall and the hills turn to dust, yet my unfailing love for you shall never be shaken." *Isaiah 54*

We can depend on the love of our God, and it will never ever let us down. Let these words feed you with God's reassurance and serenity.

22 "My word will not return to me empty, but will accomplish what I desire and achieve the purpose for which I sent it." *Isaiah 55*

We only ever see a tiny part of God's plan at any one time, and from such a viewpoint, many things seem impossible or difficult to understand. These words remind us that God is fully in control, and ultimately all shall be well.

23 "Yet, O Lord, you are our Father. We are the clay, you are the potter." *Isaiah 64*

As you think over the implications of these words, allow yourself to be molded into the kind of shape God the potter wants you to be.

24 The Lord says: "I called but you did not answer, I spoke but you did not listen." *Isaiah 65*

How often we are so busy talking and filling our minds with trivial things, that we do not notice the Lord shouting at the top of his voice, let alone whispering in a still small voice. We need to be attentive; then we will hear him.

25 The Lord says, "I will take your heart of stone and give you a heart of flesh." *Ezekiel 11*

There is no doubt that God is able to turn us into completely loving people, sensitive to other people's needs and capable of responding to them with warmth. But we do need to want it that way.

26 "I will put my Spirit in you and you will live." *Ezekiel 37*

The God we worship is the source of all life. So it is only he who can give us the kind of life we long for—fulfilled and deeply happy. He can give us not mere existence, but rich, abundant life.

27 "God gives wisdom to the wise and knowledge to the discerning. He reveals deep and hidden things." *Daniel 2*

It should be obvious that the God of wisdom can give us understanding and discernment. Yet often when our lives are confused, we spend very little time in his company, drawing wisdom from him.

28 "I will heal their waywardness and love them freely." *Hosea 14*

The lovely thing about our God is that he never gives up on us, and we can always turn back to find him opening his arms to us in love.

29 "I will pour out my Spirit on all people." *Joel 2*

Our God is so generous to us, and so long-suffering. His Spirit is not going to be dripped out, drop by drop, but poured out on all people. And "all people" means that you are one of them!

30 "In my distress I called to the Lord and he answered me." *Jonah 2*

Many millions, apart from Jonah, could testify to this being true. If you call to the Lord in your distress, the faithful, loving God will indeed answer you.

May

1 Water, or the lack of it, is quite literally a matter of life or death. Terrible suffering comes from thirst that for some reason cannot be quenched. Drinking our fill brings us blissful relief. There are many in our world who suffer from desperate physical thirst. There are many others who suffer an equally desperate spiritual thirst.

2 Physically we cannot survive without water. This basic, precious substance is vital to us. So as to ensure that our bodies get the water they need, they provide us with feelings of thirst. The more severe our need of water, the more powerful our thirst becomes. The whole point of thirst is that it drives us to find water, so we can drink and be satisfied.

3 Thirst is such a universal and powerful experience that it is often used to describe a deep spiritual longing—even craving—for satisfaction and fulfillment. What do you thirst for in your life at the moment?

4 Jesus says, paradoxically, that those who thirst for righteousness are blessed. Can such thirst really be a blessing to us? It certainly isn't comfortable. But if our thirst alerts us to our desperate need for righteousness, then it will indeed be a blessing, because it will drive us to drink from the source of righteousness, until our needs are satisfied and our spiritual thirst quenched.

5 The psalmist speaks of our need for God in terms of thirst: "God, you are my God. I pine for you; my heart thirsts for you, my body longs for you, as a land parched, dreary and waterless." *Psalm 63*

6 Unless we are aware of our thirst for God — our total need of him for our well-being and wholeness — we shall never seek him out with urgency. And unless we seek him out, we shall never discover how totally satisfying God is.

7 As we begin to be aware of our thirst for God, we shall find ourselves thirsting for those things that are part of his nature and close to his heart. Our God is a God of justice; we cannot thirst for God without thirsting and striving toward a just society.

8. Our God is a God of peace; we cannot thirst for God without thirsting for peace, and being prepared to take an active role in bringing this about, both in ourselves and our relationships, and also in the context of our society.

9. Our God is a God of compassion and forgiveness. So we cannot thirst for God without also thirsting for compassion and forgiveness in our world. And that must begin with ourselves.

10. Whenever we pray, "May your kingdom come," we are expressing our thirst for the world to be governed God's way, according to his will and in keeping with his nature.

11. There are many who thirst instead for their own kingdom to be established, for their own will to be done and their personal whims gratified. It is not only the well-known despots of the world who thirst for power. Such a thirst may be much closer to us than we like to think—in particular areas and relationships of our own lives.

12 Many thirsts that people have—for immediate gratification, for comfort, for fame—are actually a thirst for God that has not yet gone far enough. They acknowledge dissatisfaction with the present state of things, and express a deep longing to be personally valuable and filled with inner peace.

13 Disillusion and cynicism set in when people find that none of the things they thirst for actually quenches their thirst. In our society we see the result of this—a kind of "panic buying" of increasingly complex or bizarre forms of distraction so as to stave off that thirst at any cost.

14 "Be still and know that I am God." *Psalm 46*
The truth is that we do not need to invent distractions to stave off our thirst; there is a source of living water that is freely available to us, and will satisfy even those needs in us that other drinks do not touch, however expensive, frothy, or highly decorated they may be.

15 The voice of Jesus calls out to us across the centuries, loud and clear: "If anyone is thirsty, let him come to me and drink. Whoever believes in me, as the scripture has said, streams of living water will flow from within him."

16 With such an offer, why on earth do we expend such energy trying to quench our thirst in shallow puddles that will quickly run dry, when we can come to Jesus and drink freely from a source that will never dry up or turn bitter.

17 So how does Jesus satisfy our thirst? One of our basic human thirsts is to be loved for what we are. So much of our image-creating stems from the fear that we are not really lovable in our natural state, and must pretend we are different if we are to be accepted by others. With Jesus, the need for image is gone; he loves you and accepts you just as you are.

18 The thirst for fame is really a recognition that in a crowded, impersonal society, we don't feel "special." We may crave fame, thinking that if we are famous, people will notice we are special. Yet sadly, the famous are often left with a deep sense of loneliness—the opposite of what they hoped for. But our God has created you specially to be you; no matter how many others there are, *you* are infinitely precious!

19 Often it is peace of mind we thirst for. This seems to be promised by financial security, and a whole cocoon of strategies we string around ourselves. Yet we always know that if and when any of these let us down, our peace of mind will be gone. But if we place our security in the faithful, unchanging, and loving God, our peace of mind will no longer be dependent on our bank balance; our thirst will be quenched.

20 Many thirst to be rich. Partly this is linked with the desire for financial security, partly with the need for personal fulfillment—and you can see how the word "fulfillment" could be seen to mean having lots of possessions. Jesus, the source of living water, enriches our lives so that we are able to possess the greatest treasures of all—and keep them even through death into eternity.

21 We can taste and see that God is good. When we come to him with our thirst, his living water provides us with all we need. So if we come to him battered and weary from loving in difficult circumstances, for instance, we shall find the water from his well tastes of comfort and encouragement.

22 If we come to Jesus confused and frightened, we shall find that his streams of living water taste of calm, inner peace, and reassurance. He always provides us with what we need.

23 If we come to Jesus in pain or weakness, we shall find that the living water he gives us to drink tastes to us of inner strength and serenity.

24 The woman said, "Sir, give me this water!" In some ways the woman didn't understand what she was asking, and sometimes we don't, either. But Jesus never turns us away, no matter where we are, or how long we have been there. It is our longing—our thirst—that draws us to where we can be satisfied.

25 We have seen that the water of life is essential to our spiritual survival, let alone our growth. It also cleanses us, washing away all the guilt and shame of our sin. We can come to Jesus at any time for such bathing; there is no need for us to stagger through life covered with guilt. Let the Lord of Love wash you and restore you to wholeness.

26 When Jesus went to wash Peter's feet, Peter at first refused. "Lord," he exclaimed, "you shall never wash my feet!" Jesus our Lord also approaches us, his disciples, with his bowl of water and a towel tied around his waist. Do we allow our Lord to minister to us?

27 Jesus's reply to Peter is also true for us: "Unless I wash you, you have no part with me." The Lord whom we worship insists that to be with him we must allow him to minister to us as a servant. And when we pride ourselves on our independence, that is often very hard for us to accept.

28 Having washed the disciples' feet, Jesus tells them to act in the same way to one another. That teaching also refers to us. We are never to stand on our dignity or rank, but rather consider it a privilege to act as servants to one another, however menial the task. Following Christ is a practical business.

29 Water is the perfect example of recycling! Down through the ages it rains, gets used to water the earth and make things grow, evaporates, condenses into clouds, and rains again. Through the prophet Isaiah God uses such rain as an illustration of his word: "So is my word that goes out of my mouth—it will not return to me empty, but will accomplish what I desire and achieve the purpose for which I sent it."

30 When it next rains, look at it as a picture of God's generous love that is poured out on us so that we can grow and flourish.

31 Fruit trees and vines need regular watering. A thorough dousing followed by long periods of drought will stunt growth. Spiritually, too, we need to make sure that we are planted where the source of living water is, and where we can benefit from our God's refreshing rain.

June

1 During this month we shall be looking at the flowering that goes on in prayerful lives. Through the media, we are often force-fed the sad and bad side of people; spend time today thinking of all those loyal and loving prayerful ones all over our world as God's huge meadow full of flowers.

2 In a flowering meadow, what delights you first is the very natural beauty of it. Nothing is particularly arranged; flowers grow wherever the seeds happen to have taken root. Yet it is this very random, unforced flowering that adds to the fresh, natural grace of a meadow. And so it is spiritually as well. God's meadow is about people flowering wherever they happen to be planted, in a natural, unforced way.

3 Meadows of wild flowers are always so colorful. We need never fear that as we become closer to God we may lose the "natural" color of our characters. Rather the opposite—God never saps our color, but appreciates it and allows it the freedom to bloom.

4. Along with the colors of meadow flowers, we notice the huge variety there. This is all part of the richness. We should rejoice and delight in the differences between us, rather than seeing them as a threat. When we long for unity, let's not confuse that with uniformity. Let's enjoy the God-given variety of characters, which is bound to result in different colors, shapes, and forms of worship and praise. The important thing is to recognize that we are all in the same meadow!

5. Don't waste time wishing you could flower somewhere else. Enjoy flowering right here, where your seed has been planted. If you don't, there will just be an empty patch that only you can fill.

6. Don't waste time wishing you were a different plant, either. God has created you the perfect plant for the life he wants you to lead. So enjoy and appreciate the other varieties around you by all means, but don't let that turn into jealousy or covetousness. Bloom in all your own beauty and enjoy being what you are.

7. Jesus drew our attention to the way meadow flowers are so beautiful, yet they don't worry and get anxious about their clothes. We need to take this to heart—God our Father knows our needs, and we really can trust him to look after us. Knowing this to be true will free us to live abundantly.

8. We may find our own spiritual flowers surprise us. They may not bloom into what we expected or planned at all. That is part of the fun of living in the company of our God, who is full of surprises and has a remarkable sense of humor!

9. Our flowers are the first result of our spiritual growth as we are rooted and nourished by the one true God. They are more noticeable than stalks and leaves, and we need to be prepared for the fact that the more we live and grow in Christ, the more noticeable our faith will be to others. It may well be that others notice it long before we do ourselves.

10 There is in our society a kind of false humility that is embarrassed at the thought of recognizing any good in ourselves. If you notice yourself or those around you "flowering" with the natural happiness of being rooted in love, then be pleased about it, because it's wonderful! You didn't do it just by your own efforts, did you? We can enjoy working in harmony with the Lord our God.

11 Spiritual flowering can be a sign of encouragement to us and to those around us, for all these individually flowering plants bear witness to the strong root growth out of sight, to the nourishment, to the light and the watering.

12 Flowers are the first hint of fruit; the first indication that the plant is growing to maturity. Spiritually speaking, they are all those quiet, unpretentious acts of kindness, thoughtfulness, and love that result from us being made new in Christ. They start to happen naturally as our characters are "full-filled" with the loving nature of God.

13 Flowers take many shapes and colors. Our flowers may be that we shall find ourselves reacting less anxiously to problems, feeling more tolerant or less critical; we may find ourselves a little better at listening wholeheartedly, thinking ahead to save someone trouble, or thinking of a good idea that will give someone help or encouragement.

14 The flowers that any plant produces are a natural expression of that particular kind of plant. So it is with us, spiritually. We shall only ever produce signs of our life in Christ that are natural to us, so we need not feel we have to try incredibly hard in life to do what is right. If instead we open ourselves up to let God work in us, we shall gradually become good quite naturally. "A good tree cannot produce bad fruit."

15 One danger of having flowers is that we may like them so much that we start to think they are an end in themselves. This is how the rather derogatory expression "do-gooder" comes about—when the acts of kindness are done for their own sake or for self-gratification.

16 All that we are, and all we produce as a result of living in Christ, is entirely for the glory of God, and we must not try to snatch at that glory for ourselves, or we shall find that we are no longer safely rooted in the Lord of Love.

17 We can learn wisdom from the flowers God has created. In common with all his creation, they are like reflections of his nature. Think how the sunflower turns throughout the day to gaze at the sun. That steady, faithful gazing at God through the whole day is a lovely picture of constant prayer.

18 Daisies (the name used to be "day's eye") open their petals wide to receive sunlight, but close up to darkness. Whenever we see them, they can remind us to open up to God's light, and be closed to evil.

19 Roses, with their rich color and scent, are always associated with love. As you look at them and smell them, be thankful for the loveliness of our redeeming God, who is so generous with his gifts and to whom you are so special.

20 Lilies are associated with purity, often considered a rather unfashionable word at the moment. Yet it is purity that lies behind all integrity and justice; it is purity that lays the foundation for fair dealing and trust in relationships.

21 The blossoms of fruit trees, particularly in an orchard, speak to us of the profusion and generosity of God. They are also like a visual shout of praise!

22 One of the old country names for the horse chestnut tree was "candle tree," and you can easily see why when the tree is covered in great thick blossom candles of white or pink near Ascension time. That is how we could be—standing tall in the faith, with every part of us proclaiming the light of God's glory.

23 In contrast to the great chestnut trees, violets speak of the quiet and often unnoticed goodness of many beautiful Christian lives. Those who do notice them and look more closely, find intricately formed, richly colored flowers with a lovely perfume. It is a privilege to meet such people, and their gentleness is inspiring.

24 Another flower noticeable for its perfume as well as its appearance is the honeysuckle. It attracts many visitors. Churches full of loving people also attract visitors—people are drawn to Jesus through being loved there.

25 On windswept hillsides the fragile-looking bluebell manages to survive, partly because it is so flexible and light. We may sometimes feel fragile as storms howl around us. We need to remember that the Lord has promised that we will never be tried more than we are able, and since he knows our needs, we can trust him to provide us with the resources to withstand the storms we face.

26 Poppies, with their papery scarlet petals, colonized the fields of Flanders after the terrible battle there in the First World War. They remain forever a symbol to remind us of the suffering we inflict on one another, and the vulnerability of our life here. In Christ we have the assurance that our life does not end with death, and the dead whom we love, and miss, are alive through Christ in the light of eternity.

27 Dandelions get everywhere, and I know they drive gardeners crazy! But do look at them sometime when the sun shines on them—they positively glow. That kind of radiance, scattered all over the place, bringing brightness to the dirtiest places—that is what we should be like, spreading the Good News.

28 Thistles, left to grow tall and flower, can remind us that flowers can happen in the most prickly of situations, if we give them time.

29 The blue and white veronica flowers hug the ground in the fields, so that if they are accidentally trampled on by an unsuspecting cow, they can quickly perk up again. I think they have much to tell us about perseverance in the face of difficulties.

30 All flowers are shortlived and must die away for the plant to produce its fruit, yet for all that, they are incredibly detailed, intricate works of art, perfectly colored and shaped for their particular habitat and needs. Take time to look at some of them more closely, because they do reflect the glory of God.

July

1 God causes his sun to shine each day on both the evil and the good. Jesus uses this as an example of his Father's amazing love, and tells us that, if we want to behave like true children of God, we shall have to let our love shine both on our friends and also on our enemies. Without grudging the cost.

2 Since the sun's light and warmth are so important to our survival, they can help us discover a lot about God's light and warmth—in other words, his love. For they have much in common, and in many ways the life system God has created materially, reflects the spiritual life system, which springs entirely from the source of all Love.

3 Whenever you wander in the sun and enjoy it warming you through, let that pleasure and comfort lead you on to thankfulness and praise for the warmth and delight of our God's love. We can bask in his love as our bodies enjoy basking in the warm sun.

4 In the old folk story of the battle between the sun and the north wind, it is the sun's gentle warmth that persuades the man to take his cloak off—the strong, cold wind just made him wrap his cloak around him more tightly. If you find that you are facing a particularly obstinate situation, give up on the harsh, cold, and bitter approach. Try the warmth of love instead. You will find that it works.

5 Love is so effective that even the hard world of business has tried to cash in on it. Top managerial conferences now often include advice to show interest in people, and look after them, because that makes them feel wanted, and happy people work harder!

6 We could easily become very cynical about the way businesses are trying to mimic love for profit. Or we can learn from it, much as Jesus suggested we learn from the unjust steward—if even pretending to love makes people money, then how much more will our world gain if we practice the real thing?

7 Many flowers begin to open up as they feel light and warmth shining on them. So do we. In so many difficult relationships the warmth of love has the power to open people up to one another again, as trust is restored.

8 Jesus said that perfect love casts out fear. It is fear that makes us build up those huge barricades around ourselves for protection, fear that prompts us to get in our defensive aggression before the other person has a chance! What is it that we all fear so much? We fear attack on our survival, not just physical survival, but that precious tangle of character, dreams, and awareness that is "Me" and no one else. This we love, and will defend at all cost.

9 In Gethsemane Jesus prayed, "Father, if it is possible, let this cup pass from me; nevertheless, let your will, not mine, be done." If we really want God's will to be done in us, we shall have to loosen our grip on our life's "ownership." Dare we do that?

10 When we relinquish that tight hold on our life, and entrust ourselves to the God who loves us, then our "preservation-at-all-costs" attitude can be relaxed, and we need no longer keep rushing to our own defense.

11 Defenses are not necessary if we belong to the One who has already won the victory over evil. As Paul says in his letter to the Romans, "If God is for us, who can be against us?"

12 The love that comes from God is warm, comforting, and gentle; it is also powerful like fire and we would be fools to underestimate its strength.

13 God burns with so great a love for us that he laid aside his majesty, accepted vulnerablity, and broke into his own creation in order to save us and reconcile us to himself.

14 We know from our own human relationships how precious love feels, and history is full of the acts of courage, selflessness, and greatness that have been inspired by love through the ages. Love seems to awaken us to being fully human. That is not really surprising because love is the ground of our being.

15 "Dear friends, let us love one another, for love comes from God. Everyone who loves has been born of God and knows God."
1 John 4:7–8

16 As we enjoy the light and warmth of God's love, the power of that love gets to work in us, until we start to shine with reflective light, becoming lights for others in the process.

17 We can see the love of God most clearly in action in the person of Jesus. It is Jesus's way to love people to wholeness, with no ulterior motives and no strings attached. Dare we believe that he really loves us with such completeness?

18 Jesus's love is full of compassion and understanding for people, even when their needs are thrust at him when he is about to go and rest. How far does our loving reflect such love?

19 Jesus's love for people shares so deeply in their pain that he can see their hurts and fears behind their masks, and reach out to them regardless of their social, educational, or cultural background. How far does our loving reflect such love?

20 Jesus's love reaches out and touches people, even where it would be better for his image if he ignored them, even when his friendship with them earns him contempt. How far does our loving reflect such love?

21 Jesus's love forgives those who are deliberately causing him pain, those who are tearing him and his followers apart, and those whom he thought he could trust. How does *our* love compare?

22 In the light of such love, is our own meager loving too thin and scant to count as love? Certainly it is the real stuff, and God rejoices over every spark of love we show. "No one has ever seen God; but if we love one another, God lives in us and his love is made complete in us." *1 John 4:12*

23 Jesus accepted the small offering of five loaves and two fish, and with it fed 5000 people. Even the smallest, truly loving act on our part is like an offering that our God can use for great good.

24 Since we are commanded to love one another, we do not have to wait until we feel like it before we dive in.

25 There may be times when our love and forgiveness toward someone are so fragile that we can only love by doing something kind. Our hearts take longer to catch up. They may not yet feel like loving at all. Such acts are not in any way false; they will be preparing the way for the time when we can actually feel love once again.

26 If you are finding it hard to forgive someone, ask God to increase your love for them. Many times each day, thank him for loving both you and this person. At first you will even find it hard to say such a thing. But gradually, God's love will melt your heart and enable you to forgive and be free.

27 Pray with particular care for those you find it difficult to get on with. Both you and they are in need of God's healing love.

28 We cannot hope to reflect the light and warmth of God's love effectively unless we are turned to face it. If we spend most of our time with our minds turned toward worldly things, then these are the things that our lives will reflect.

29 "Do not conform any longer to the pattern of this world, but be transformed by the renewing of your mind." *Romans 12:2*

30 The fire of God's love can refine and purify. Before we can be fully indwelled by the Lord of Love, all that is evil in us must be destroyed. Before God's kingdom can be totally established on earth as in heaven, all evil in the universe must be destroyed. The last enemy to be destroyed is death.

31 The great Good News of our faith is that Love has shown in Jesus that it is stronger than death, and is indeed victorious over evil. "Be of good cheer," says Jesus, "I have overcome the world!"

August

1 With the ground prepared, and with strong root systems established, plants have been growing. Nourished and watered, they have flowered. Throughout the warmth of the summer the fruit has been swelling, and now that fruit is ripening. Every year this slow rhythm of growth and fruiting happens, like a living picture of our own spiritual growth and fruiting.

2 Through the prophet Jeremiah, the Lord announces that those who trust and are rooted in him are like trees planted beside streams of water, greatly blessed and bearing fruit even in years of drought.

3 The fruit we are called to bear is not the occasional silver nutmeg or golden pear. It is real, nourishing fruit, and the crop keeps coming in increasing abundance with each successive year.

4. Bearing spiritual fruit is sometimes confused with working all out for those one-off performances in our own strength, which leave us drained and exhausted, with a distinct horror of fruiting again! Relax, because real spiritual fruiting will happen quite naturally, and cannot be forced.

5. Look after your roots and your fruits will look after themselves.

6. Jesus teaches us that the fruit we produce in our lives will be a direct result of the kind of plant we are. We don't expect to find figs on thorn bushes, or grapes on brambles, and it's the same with people—good spiritual fruit will not grow from a bad tree; on the other hand, a good tree will quite naturally produce good fruit.

7. On several occasions, Paul tried listing the various spiritual fruits. First on the list comes love. We cannot ever spend enough time meditating on this amazing quality, so fundamental to the character of the God we adore, and so essential in our own lives and in our world. Everyone who loves must have roots in God's love. Anyone without love cannot be rooted in God.

8 The next spiritual fruit is joy. This doesn't mean either empty, set smiles or callous rejoicing that is oblivious to suffering. Joy is the sense of celebration that infuses everything—even pain and distress—when we know with surety that God is in all things and Love is in control.

9 Joy is the sense of lighthearted freedom that comes from knowing God is with us, no matter what strange or hostile surroundings we happen to be in, and no matter how badly we may be treated for doing what we know is right in God's eyes. Joy is the realization that nothing at all can ever separate us from the love of God that is in Christ Jesus, our Lord.

10 Peace is closely linked with joy. Jesus never promised us a worldly type of peace, but he offers us something far better and far more satisfying—his own peace. As his followers we shall find it impossible to lead a comfortable, well-insulated life, but we shall know the deep, inner tranquility of being at one with the God of Love, who made us.

11 Patience is spiritual fruit as well. That comes as good news to those of us who do not possess a great deal of it in our basic makeup! If it is fruit of the Spirit, then it must increase in us through the power of God working in us and transforming us.

12 It is impossible to force something like patience. When impatient people are trying really hard not to explode, the tension is terrific, and there's no way this determined tightness can be called "patience"! Patience, like faith, is not so much to do with determined effort, as letting go. It will only start to happen once we recognize that we are not in control of the universe, and the world will not fall apart if things don't happen exactly as and when we think they should.

13 Kindness is like one of those color filters you can put on a camera lens for a particular effect, because it colors the way we do things — right through from smallest, briefest encounters, to the most significant acts of our lives.

14 Kindness expresses care and reverence for someone, and will show as much in the way we act in stores, or while traveling, as it will when we are making wedding arrangements or looking after someone who is chronically ill. And true kindness carries on regardless of being appreciated.

15 Goodness is a fruit that is deeply valued, yet often publicly scorned. There is a great human thirst for a trustworthy goodness in people, in politics, and in all society, but it is coupled with the seeming hopelessness of ever finding it. So we react by laughing at our absurd, impossible longing and distrust what looks like goodness for fear it will smash our hopes by proving false.

16 Like seaside rock, Goodness has got to have "genuine" rolled into it all the way through. For it is that lasting quality in someone that marks them out to be full of integrity, with nothing false or bitter or cruel or self-seeking about them. Goodness is like refined gold.

17 Faithfulness is an immensely reassuring and comforting fruit. Slow to mature and mellow, unpretentious and easily overlooked, it is most often noticed when absent—when it is there we tend to take it for granted.

18 Faithfulness is a fruit that puts quite a demand on a plant's resources, owing to its constant fruiting habit. It can therefore only happen in plants that have their roots firmly embedded near the constant flow of God's living water. Faithfulness tastes particularly sweet during times of drought.

19 Gentleness involves sensitivity. It has nothing to do with the rather scrawny, ineffectual cartoon image of priests at garden parties—determinedly mild and anxious never to offend. Gentleness actually stems from controlled strength, rather like a powerful orchestra playing a beautiful passage very softly so as to bring out the full meaning of it.

20 Gentleness is listening to the needs of others beneath their outward behavior and responding to that often disguised cry of pain or loneliness. Gentleness is holding others in reverence, so that we do not crash in on them and inadvertently snuff out a smoldering wick, or break a bruised reed.

21 Self-control first needs to admit that the self needs controlling! In our world it is acceptable—even praiseworthy—to indulge ourselves and do whatever comes naturally to our desires. I'm afraid this is one area where we are bound to clash with society if we are living in Christ, because in his law of Love, self-control is a must.

22 The core of Jesus's teaching—"Love God and love your neighbor"—requires that our own feelings and wishes no longer rule our actions. Whenever we consider God and our neighbor before ourselves, we are controlling self-centered behavior. Bear in mind, though, that if selfless actions are done in a resentful, grudging spirit, they will lack love, and profit us nothing. Without love, the fruit of self-control turns bitter; with love, it is fragrant and sweet.

23 In all these fruits of the Spirit we can see that love is the center, love is the source, and love is the result. Fruit-bearing Christians will, through their behavior, be spreading love in a tired and confused world, thirsty for worth and meaning.

24 It is so important to keep reminding ourselves that fruit is not just there to look at, but also to feed. The Dead Sea lacks life because so many mineral riches flow into it, but there are no outlets. Overripe, unpicked blackberries start to decay, infecting even those fruits in the same cluster that have not yet ripened. It is vital that we allow our fruit to be picked and "eaten."

25 We can enjoy fruiting. Even a quick glance at our created universe shows us that God delights in abundant, colorful, exuberant life. Made in his image, we naturally delight in seeing good produced—it makes us happy to be creative. I am quite sure that the Lord of Creation loves us to share that joy, and rejoices with us.

26 Not all fruits are succulent and sweet. It may be that sometimes we produce good fruit that we do not recognize as such because it is born of deep hurt and suffering, grief, or rejection. The fact is that some fruit hurts to produce, but it is precious and nourishing for all that.

27 Think of a great walnut tree, huge and heavy with fruit. The walnuts are hard and wrinkled, with tough shells. But that fruit is delicious, nutritious, and versatile. Spiritual fruit produced in the dark times of our life may feel hard and wrinkled to us. It too may have a hard shell. But it is good fruit, and can be well used for the good of the world.

28 Fruit takes time to ripen, and so do fruits of the Spirit. Don't try to rush your fruit. Jesus said, "I am the true vine, my Father is the gardener"; trust the Lord, then, to bring you to fruit at the right time. In the meantime, enjoy the growing.

29 Not all plants fruit at the same time. Do not be jealous if you see others fruiting when you are going through a time of hidden growth. There are times in our lives when we need to be on the receiving end, and many of us find it hard to accept care from others. Yet accepting is in itself a fruit—the fruit of humility.

30 Jesus has warned us that every fruiting branch will be pruned so that it will become more fruitful. When you find yourself being pruned, then, consider it a special privilege.

31 If we remain in Christ and Christ in us, we shall bear much fruit; dead, withered branches, parted from Christ, bear no fruit at all, and are only good for burning. Take care that you remain rooted in the Lord of Love, and don't try fruiting on your own.

September

1 Having fruited, we must allow ourselves to be harvested. This may sound obvious, and you would think that having got this far we would long to be harvested and used. Yet the struggle against growing for our own glory—growing for ourselves—continues even into harvest.

2 Unless we are very careful we can get choosy about who is going to benefit from our fruit, and hold on to it tightly until it is picked by someone we approve of. Are we so courteous and respectful to those we dislike as to those we admire, for instance? And do we have limitless patience in our work, but very little in our own family?

3 When our fruit is noticed, and people praise us for it, do we allow it to be harvested by passing the glory on to its rightful source—God himself? If we accept the praise for ourselves, and bask in the glory that belongs to the Lord, the fruit will vanish and our growing will be wasted. Worse still, we shall have failed to feed others with the love that God has entrusted to us.

4. Holding on to our fruit happens when we forget that we have relinquished ownership to the Lord of Love. Fruit may grow on us, but we are only stewards of it, not owners any more. If much fruit has been produced in us, much will be required of us.

5. Often God will set us fruiting in places and at times that we probably would never have chosen. But we can trust the God of Faithfulness with the details of our fruiting. All we are to do is to make ourselves available, so we can be in the right place with the right people at the right time for the kingdom to grow.

6. Sometimes we are wary of agreeing to a task we sense God is calling us to do, because we feel inadequate and ill-equipped for it. It is as if we are being harvested before we feel the fruit is ripe. Don't be afraid; the Lord knows you well, and loves you well, and he will never ask you more than you are able, in his strength, to give.

7 It may be that as your fruit is harvested you are surprised at the quality of the fruit God has produced in you. Perhaps a situation arises where you find yourself able to cope using patience, self-control, or inner peace you had not realized you possessed. Give thanks to God, and delight in the joy of working in harmony with your Lord.

8 Harvesting can make us aware of our weakness. Jesus knew when the woman in the crowd had touched him hoping for healing, because at that moment he felt strength going out of him.

9 It may be that when demands are being made on us, and we feel weakened by them, that is when the Lord is using those fruits he has produced in us. Do not complain at such times, then, but rejoice that your prayer to be used is being answered. Temporary weakness is all part of the privilege.

10 Never forget that you can draw new strength from the source of all life and wholeness. The Lord offers you freely as much as you want, whenever you need it. You have only to ask.

11 Sometimes we find that through being harvested, more fruit is growing. Our faith may grow through being tested; through practicing gentleness in one particular area of our life, we may find ourselves growing in gentleness toward someone we previously found it hard to love.

12 Walnut trees are shaken to be harvested. It may be that our spiritual fruits emerge when our lives are shaken in some way. Shaking may be unsettling and disturbing, but it can also release God's fruit in us, and become a very productive experience.

13 We can also think of ourselves as being the harvest—part of the living bread that is the body of Christ. In typical human style, we do not always take kindly to being harvested, even when we have prayed for God to use our lives. As soon as we start being ground into flour we begin our complaining and questioning.

14 So often we want the pleasure of ripening to golden grain, without the pain of being ground into flour for making bread. Yet that is the only way the world can be fed. We can only be God's bread if we are willing, first of all, to become flour.

15 Jesus prepared us for the inevitability of our being broken so that the world can be fed. He tells us that it is a great blessing to be insulted and persecuted because of our life in him, and suggests we rejoice and be glad as soon as this starts to happen!

16 Although we have been warned about being broken, in order to be useful, it usually comes as a shock, and up to the surface bubbles all our righteous indignation: "Why did you bother making me this nice golden grain shape, if you're only going to grind me into powder? I thought you promised to keep me safe—why are you letting this happen?" and so on.

17 The Lord says nothing in reply to our indignant accusations, any more than he replied to those who jeered at him as he hung in weakness on the cross. But it is here we have our answer: the harvest of complete love was complete weakness and seeming destruction at the hand of his enemies. It is the only way for Love to win over evil; it is the only way to bring about full and everlasting life.

18 It is a mark of great honor to be allowed the privilege of sharing Christ's suffering. Once we think of any hardship in this light it loses its power to destroy, releasing instead a strange sensation of joy, right there in the mess of the pain.

19 Harvesting also involves spreading the fruit around so that many can benefit from the crop. Jesus annoyed some of the religious people by spending time with the outcasts and sinners. But he pointed out that he had come for those who needed healing (and who knew their need of healing).

20 It is quite a temptation for us to become so involved in "church life" that we have no time left to be fruiting among those who think they would never darken the doors of a church, but whose hunger for the Unknown God is very great. Yet if we do not reach them, who will?

21 Jesus saw the great numbers of souls with longing in their hearts and emptiness in their lives, and urged his disciples to ask God to send many workers to harvest this precious "crop." You are among those who have been sent in answer to that prayer.

22 Most of those brought to the Lord have turned toward him in the first place as a direct result of knowing a Christian whose love for God fills his or her life. Are you in contact with someone who does not yet know the Lord?

23 I have said that we fruit naturally—that we will naturally behave lovingly if we are rooted in the Lord of Love. But we sometimes try to disguise or hide God's fruit when we are with those who do not believe. Perhaps we are concerned not to thrust our faith down their necks; perhaps we try to protect the Lord from insult. Do not hide it—share the treasure you have found. You may be the only person who can bring them to know God's love for themselves.

24 Jesus called Peter the fisherman to harvest people for God, instead of harvesting fish. One of the first important occasions when Peter began to do this was at Pentecost, when, freshly filled with God's Spirit, he led the disciples running out into the street and excitedly proclaimed the Good News to the crowds about Jesus being the promised Savior. Delivering the Good News is a vital part of harvesting for God.

25 Do we know enough about our faith to be able to share it with others when the occasion arises?

26 When we are workers in God's harvest, we can only harvest using methods and equipment given to us by the Lord of the harvest. Above all, we are not to drive people into the kingdom, but love them there.

27 As we share the treasure of God's Good News, we must start, as Jesus always does, at the point a person is at now. That means no set speeches or watertight, inflexible programs. Our personal God loves each one as an individual, with particular needs and luggage. If we are to work with this God, we too must work person-to-person.

28 Our loving God's concern is with wholeness for his children, and that includes the body, the mind, and the emotions as well as the spirit. So when we join him as workers in the harvest, that must be our concern as well—practical, all-around concern that is never suddenly withdrawn, but continues to be given, whether the person is easy and likable, or covered in inconvenient prickles.

29 We need to remember all the time that it is the Lord's harvest we are working on—not our own. While we keep this truth in our hearts, the harvesting will be a truly joyful business, no matter what setbacks we face and no matter how long it takes.

30 The completion of the harvest will be the day when Christ returns in all God's glory, and everything in all time and place will be brought to full accomplishment. With great hope and joy we can look forward to the coming of that glorious day.

October

1 With its early mists and mellow sunlight, this month is valuable as a time for reflection and quietness. Jesus would walk off into the hills to spend hours alone with his Father during his ministry on earth. And he recognized in Martha's sister, Mary, the value of time spent sitting and listening.

2 Sit at the feet of Jesus and listen to him.

3 Being in reflective stillness with God does not necessarily mean waiting for a place where there is no noise or activity going on. If we waited for that, we'd wait forever! God is Lord of the real, fussy, noisy world, and we can find his stillness right in the middle of the everyday chaos.

4 Hear the noises around you, acknowledge them, and put them to one side. They provide a practical backdrop to the still presence of our real, living, practical God. You will even find that rather than distracting you from him, they can emphasize the peace of his presence within you.

5. Sometimes we are suddenly made aware of God's power of stillness, close and personal. It may be a very brief sensation, or last longer, but either way we know we have been met and touched with his love, and the memory of such times is very precious.

6. We may find ourselves in moments of communion with the Lord through a sense of wonder at something in his creation. It may come from our delight in something beautiful, innocent, touching, or skillful. When we expect such moments, and keep our spiritual eyes open, we are more likely to notice them.

7. Being tuned in to God's moments of stillness is a habit we can cultivate. Most of the time we go about so preoccupied that we are quite unobservant about anything unexpected—if we're not expecting to see something we just don't notice it. It is when we walk through the days expecting to see God's footprints, that we begin to see clearly where his feet pass.

8 "This is my Son, whom I love." These are the words spoken by the voice from heaven at Jesus's baptism, and they are beautiful words to reflect on during the day. The Spirit of God, gentle as a dove, is reassuring and strengthening Jesus in his human weakness, confirming the truth about him and anointing him for the task before him.

9 "I formed you . . . I shall not forget you." These words, spoken through the prophet Isaiah to Israel, are spoken also to you today. The love God has for you is like that of a loving parent, only deeper and more complete even than that.

10 "Jesus's teaching made a great impression on them because, unlike the scribes, he taught them with authority." As you reflect on these words, recognize in Jesus the human face of God.

11 When the man with leprosy came and fell at Jesus's feet, he knew that if Jesus wanted to heal him, he had the power to do it. Jesus responds warmly, not only to that leper, but to all who long to be made spiritually well: "I do want to! Be clean." *Mark 1:42*

12 Jesus replied, "Come and see." In John's gospel Andrew and another disciple tag along behind Jesus on John the Baptist's recommendation. Jesus sees them following, and when they ask him where he lives invites them to come and see. When your life is an asking to know and love Jesus more, his reply is you, too. Take him up on it.

13 "How blessed are the pure in heart: they shall see God." Reflect on these words of Jesus today. They direct us both to the perfect, loving goodness of our glorious God, and also to our own need to be transformed through his power in every part of our being.

14 "Everyone who asks, receives." In God's kingdom no one is ineligible. God's saving love and grace are available for every person, including even you. Reflect on Jesus's words and trust them.

15 "Anyone who does the will of God, that person is my brother and sister and mother." Think over the full meaning of these words; the incarnate God—Jesus Christ—is happy to consider us, the beings he has created, as close family members when we act in keeping with God's family likeness.

16 "If anyone loves me, he will obey my teaching." It is love that will make us obedient. Love for Jesus will make us long to act in accordance with his ways. And when we act in love, we shall indeed be behaving as children of the God of Love.

17 "Take courage! It's me! Don't be afraid." The disciples are terrified because they are seeing Jesus where they don't expect him to be—walking toward them on the water while they are battling against a strong wind. We need not be frightened by glimpses of God's power; that power is totally good, and tender with compassion.

18 "Do you want to get well?" Jesus is speaking to the man who has been an invalid for thirty-eight years. It may seem a strange question, but Jesus looked on the man's heart and knew the question had to be asked as part of his healing. Do we really want to be healed spiritually, when we know it will involve us changing?

19 "Your faith has healed you; go in peace." Often Jesus would say these words to those who had come to him for healing and wholeness. They are not just words, though. Jesus is God's healing Word, and his words of peace make that peace a joyful reality in our lives.

20. "He who is not with me is against me." These are sobering words to reflect on today. Unless we are actively living our lives in accordance with the Way of Jesus, we are actively working against him. Evil flourishes through the refusal of the good to work against it.

21. After an exhausting day of ministry Jesus invites his disciples to come with him to a quiet place for rest. But a huge crowd is waiting for them. What is the reaction of Jesus in his weariness? "He had compassion on them, because they were like sheep without a shepherd."

22. "He welcomed them, and spoke to them about the Kingdom of God, and healed those who needed healing." These three things are the hallmarks of Jesus's ministry, both then in Galilee and now, through his living Spirit, anywhere in the world.

23. "He who is least among you all—he is the greatest." Jesus had stood a little child in the middle of his disciples to make this point. Yet how often do we strive to be the "least"? How often do we delight in our kindness going unnoticed, or our sacrifices unacknowledged?

24 "Do not let your hearts be troubled. Trust in God: trust also in me." Let these words wash through your whole being, as you reflect on their truth and healing power.

25 "Woe to the world because of the things that cause people to sin!" Do we get so used to bad influences in our society that we start considering them acceptable? Are we active enough in protecting our young from being led astray into danger?

26 "If your hand causes you to sin, cut it off." Jesus deliberately uses strong, exaggerated images to make a point we often prefer to ignore. So much sin is caused by us courting temptation. Jesus's teaching is quite clear—cut yourself off from what is tempting you to sin at the first opportunity. Don't play with temptation.

27 "God has come to help his people." This was the Good News that people gossiped to others after Jesus had brought to life the widow's son at Nain. Reflect on it today—it is so amazing, and yet so true.

28 "Where two or three come together in my name, there am I with them." What a wonderful promise this is. We should revere it and never take it for granted. Do we always acknowledge the real presence of the Lord at such gatherings?

29 "Anyone who will not receive the Kingdom of God like a little child will never enter it." Little children have an openness and trust that is often discarded as we grow older. Receiving God's truth as little children will mean there are no barriers of cynicism, embarrassment, dulled perception, or preconceived ideas.

30 "What is impossible with men is possible with God." So often we think of God as human-sized, or even smaller, when it comes to believing in his capacity to change things. But we are dealing with the Almighty God, who made stars and holds all things in being. With God nothing is impossible. Nothing at all.

31 "My prayer is not that you take them out of the world but that you protect them from the evil one." Just before he was arrested, Jesus prayed for all his followers. He was praying then for you. You are in the loving heart of Jesus Christ. You are in his thoughts and in his prayers. So you are perfectly safe, and perfectly loved.

November

1. As we move deeper into the autumn, and the days shorten and grow colder, we are made aware once again of the temporary nature of things in this life. Plants that sprung up so strongly in the spring are now dying back; their fresh, uncurling leaves are now yellowing and brittle. We are reminded by everything around us, that we, too, are mortal, and our time here is really quite short.

2. It is fashionable to discount thoughts about dying as unnecessarily morbid. We are encouraged to work hard at prolonging our lives, and putting off the aging process as long as possible. At the very least, we are supposed to disguise it so that it doesn't show. What are we afraid of?

3. Surely our distaste for looking older is linked with our knowledge of a truth that will not go away: getting older means we are getting uncomfortably nearer to death—the end of life. Instead of being worried by that, use it to appreciate what you have now.

4 Watching the yearly natural dying away gives us the opportunity to look at life realistically, and recognize that in fact our lives are full of small "dyings," all of which can prepare us for the main event.

5 Much of the dying away in nature happens when something has fulfilled its purpose, and so is no longer required. The flower, so necessary for attracting pollinating insects, dies away once its job is done, so that the fruit can come. When something we love in our life comes to an end, it may well be that through this dying away, something else in us is enabled to fruit.

6 As Christians, we are forever traveling on a journey—a pilgrimage to heaven. So we must expect the scenery to keep changing, with one lovely view coming to an end before we glimpse another one ahead. We need to remember, too, that the best views on a journey are usually difficult to get to, and often involve a hard climb.

7 Each time we move on to something new in our lives, we are bound to leave something behind. That, too, is like a little death, and we need to learn to accept that it happens. As we do so with the small things in life, we are being trained in accepting obedience.

8   When you have taken an important decision, don't waste time on endless regrets; whichever way you chose you would have had to leave something behind. Accept what is now; offer it for God to work through, and he will be able to make it beautiful, because he is, by trade, a redeemer.

9   Much of our dread of death comes from a deeply held belief that this life is good, and it will only last as long as our bodies hold out. The fact of the Resurrection changes that. Jesus passed through death into fullness of life, and if we are one with him, he takes us with him, through our physical death and on into the fullness of life in heaven.

10 From the way most of us behave, much of the time, an observer might infer that we consider this life far more precious and worth preserving than the fullness of heavenly life.

11 It is always best to be honest with ourselves. Perhaps we do prefer this life, because at least we are sure of it; it is familiar, and we feel at home here. And perhaps that's where storms and disasters in our lives can sometimes inadvertantly do us a favor— by reminding us of this life's temporary nature, and helping us recognize our need for a fulfillment that is not temporary but permanent.

12 Natural storms can be very violent at this time of year. For all the machinery of living with which we surround ourselves, we are still vulnerable in the face of severe winds, floods, and storms. This, too, points us to our true condition—we are weak, and we are vulnerable, however much we may try to persuade ourselves otherwise.

13 Recognizing our vulnerability can be the first step to acknowledging our dependence on God. Those of us who are particularly possessive of our independence find it almost impossible to allow God control of our lives until, at some point and for some reason, we reach the end of our own resources and strength.

14 There are countless people gripping grimly on to their independence, fearful that if they give God an inch he will exact a mile. But God is Love, not a debt collector. As soon as you give him an inch, he gives you back several miles you didn't know you had lost! And the odd thing is, that you no longer want to hoard that "independence" out of his reach.

15 Another thing we can learn from watching the natural storms is the way flexibility in the stems of plants enables them to weather severe winds. Tall grasses may look fragile, but because they bend, they survive. Dry, brittle stems get easily snapped. Like plants, we need to draw up into us the sap that keeps us spiritually supple. Are we content to walk where the Spirit of God directs us?

16 Are we only willing to hear God out if he tells us what we want to hear?

17 If it is a long time since God surprised you, perhaps you are getting spiritually rather stiff, and need to ask him to loosen you up, so that you are flexible again. Then you will notice his love and peace in all kinds of unexpected people and places.

18 Being rigid and brittle can make our worship a dry husk of habit or ritual. The life has gone out of it. Yet once real, committed praying begins again in any congregation, the sap of God's love flows through it, so that the worship becomes vibrant and beautiful. The form that worship takes hardly matters at all in comparison with this essential God-given vitality.

19 Dead worship will never be revived by anything except a fresh commitment to prayer on the part of the worshippers. No amount of gimmickry will help. Even super-efficient planning won't help on its own; refined worship is not necessarily vibrant with God's love.

20 If you, as a worshipper, pray for God to pour out his Spirit among you all, and inspire the leaders to touch the hearts of the congregation, and they to receive God's word, then life will be breathed into the most lifeless of situations, and God's Name will be truly glorified in that community.

21 The Church is the body of Christ and it is often terribly weakened by the lack of spiritual vitality in its members. In this body, every Christian's spiritual life is vital. We cannot expect to be a living, vibrant community unless we are all bound together and revived by Christ himself.

22 Paul was so happy at the thought of his future spent in the eternity of God's love, that he couldn't make up his mind which was better—to carry on living and working in this life in harmony with Jesus, or to be worshipping him in heaven forever! He would be perfectly content with either, so death was no longer anything to fear.

23 Many people worry a lot about the way the world is going, and what a terrible life it may be in ten or twenty years' time. If we didn't know about spring, we could get desperately worried about the decaying leaves of autumn. The Lord of Creation is fully in charge of all things, and we do not need to carry these burdens of anxiety. Just think—this moment now is what people were dreading some ten or twenty years ago, and it isn't so bad, is it?

24 The more we are able to live in the present, and celebrate the precious nature of each moment we are given, the less we shall worry about things that may never happen anyway.

25 A new life is what God's living Spirit gives us. A Christian community that is full of this life will be alive to the needs of the area, and attract people to seek God's face because they will see the effects of God's new life in his followers and want to have a share in that life for themselves.

26 At this time of year snow can be a menace. Obscuring our vision, it makes driving particularly hazardous. Accidents are more likely when drivers speed on even when they can't see where they are going, and spiritually we are all guilty of this. Without waiting for God's light to guide us and make our route clear, we race ahead with our own plans, often endangering others as well as ourselves in the process.

27 If your route in a particular direction is "snowbound," and seems blocked with obscurity, refuel, and wait for the snowstorm to pass.

28 When we stand in a heavy snowstorm, and nothing is visible, that doesn't mean that everything has disappeared. We know that although we can't see things, they are still there. When you next notice this, use it as a reminder of a spiritual truth: if we find ourselves going through times when we are for some reason not aware of God, it means only that we can't at the moment perceive him; it doesn't mean he isn't there.

29 Faith can only begin to deepen when the evidence is hidden from our eyes.

30 Whatever dangers or storms you have to face in your living and your dying, the God who made you and who loves you will always be at your side, closer even than thinking. And he will bring you safely to the joy of everlasting life in his presence.

December

1 December is the darkest month, with some days only just arriving at full light before the evening starts to close in. For many creatures it is a hostile, harsh, and dangerous time, with predators active, their hunting sharpened by hunger. Jesus said, "I am sending you out as sheep among wolves."

2 One of the most important qualities about our God, is that he is not only interested in us when everything is going well. He is faithful in his love for us through our very darkest days, when we are weak, vulnerable, surrounded by hostility, or under spiritual attack.

3 It is not wise to underestimate the power of evil. The last thing Satan wants is for us to grow closer to God, and increasingly like him.

4 Any glimmering of new light shining in us presents a threat to Satan's kingdom of darkness. Any increase in the Kingdom of God, with its love, peace, and joy, means that Satan's kingdom is being diminished; we are warned by Jesus that the struggle against good will get more fierce and desperate as the Kingdom of God advances.

5   So often we play into the hand of the enemy of God by our lack of vigilance, and our refusal to get actively involved in seeking good. The great human atrocities of every age do not spring up overnight—they breed from years of unchallenged greed, unhealed hatred, and uncurbed cruelty.

6   "Be self-controlled and alert," Peter warns us, "because your enemy the devil prowls around like a roaring lion looking for someone to devour. Resist him, standing firm in the faith."

7   Vigilance against evil in ourselves and in our society is essential, and we need to learn the signs of danger; so the red warning lights flash and we can take action quickly. In our own lives this may mean a sudden backtrack on what we have started to say; or a change of plans in what we have agreed to do. Don't just let yourself be drawn along as if the evil is inevitable; in the power of Christ you have the power to change things now, before it's too late.

8 If we are in the company of the Lord of Love, our vigilance will alert us to what is uncaring, unjust, and evil in society. That is good, but it will have no effect unless we become actively involved in putting things right. Make your concerns known to those in authority; write letters and support campaigns for upholding what is good and changing what is corrupt or unjust. Jesus says that those who do not gather with him are actively scattering.

9 "I want you to be wise as serpents and as innocent as doves." *Matthew 10:16*

10 Sometimes the darkness in our lives becomes so thick that it threatens to overwhelm us. Many suffer a terrible darkness from depression, grief, physical chronic pain, emotional instability, or progressively debilitating disease. Jesus knew this darkness when he was hanging on the cross; he knows and shares that awful sense of separation and loneliness, pain, and human failure. In such times he is especially close to us; we are sharing with him and he with us in the agonizing suffering of human mortality.

11 Through Christ's suffering and pain and death, came abundant life, and the great victory over evil. The Lord of Life can redeem our suffering, to bring from it abundant good. When we allow him access to our pain or grief, he can use it, and bring us to wholeness. What began as a curse can end as a blessing, both for us and for others.

12 "Even if I walk through the darkest valley I shall fear no evil, for you are with me; your rod and your staff comfort me." *Psalm 23*

13 John speaks of the way Jesus is like a light that shines in the darkness. At times we may feel there is an awful lot of darkness, but that light of the loving expression of God is never overcome by darkness—it is never quenched.

14 Gradually the light of God's love will increase in this last age, until in the fullness of light, all darkness will disappear, as night does in the light of dawn. This is the day we look toward as the Second Coming of Jesus Christ in glory.

15 The deep darkness of winter is not without hope. We know that new growth will come from this dying. For some seeds the cold and frost are a necessary stage in breaking down shells so that new life can begin. Perhaps that is spiritually true for us too.

16 As we work hard to get everything ready for the great Christmas festival, we need also to prepare ourselves spiritually to welcome the living Word into our lives at a more profound level than ever before. Our willingness to do this is the best gift we could offer.

17 Few of us would find it practical to spend extra time in prayer at this time of year, but what we can do is to use the opportunities for worship that are offered to us. For instance we can let the Christmas lights in the mall be for us a reminder to praise our God, the Light of the world. "The people who walked in darkness have seen a great light."

18 As you send your cards, and open those sent to you, commend each receiver and sender to the love of God, even if they do not yet know him. Use this opportunity to forgive more thoroughly anyone who has wronged or hurt you. Make this a time for reconciliation, accepting that you may have to make the first move. "First be reconciled to your brother, and then come and offer your gift to the Lord."

19 Let the presents you wrap be reminders of God's love for you and whomever each present is for. Thank God for your family and friends as you prepare each gift, and pray for them, asking God to pour out his spiritual gifts on their lives. "I will pour out my spirit on all flesh."

20 As you decorate your home or place of work, make this an outward sign of an inward expression of your love and thanks, to honor and praise the God of eternity. "Glory be to God in the highest!"

21 As you prepare food and drink for Christmas, bring in love to the Lord all those who will eat and drink with you over the festival. Ask God to be among you all for great good, for a deepening of love and understanding, and for joy. "Come and eat."

22 As you hear the familiar carols, be open to what the words are saying; pray them as you sing them, and allow God to speak to you through them. "O hush the noise, ye men of strife, and hear the angels sing."

23 As you plan any extra little surprises, feel at one with the Lord who enjoys giving us blessings, and surprising us with joy. Thank God for his amazing generosity to us all, and pass on the gifts he has freely given to you. "Freely you have received; freely give. Go in my Name and because you believe, others will know that I live."

24 The Light of the world stands in person at the door of your heart and knocks. Open the door to him today as never before, so that he can come in and make his home with you. Ask and you will receive.

25 With immeasureable humility, God Almighty lays aside his glory and becomes one with those he has created—dependent on their care for his human safety. Such a risk could only be taken by One whose love was without limit. "The light of Christ has come into the world."

26 Commit to the Lord of Love any gatherings you are joining over this time, and all the conversations you will be having. Our task is to make ourselves available to God so that we can be used anywhere at any time. So keep in close touch with the Lord of your life. And Mary replied, "Let it happen to me as you have said."

27 The darkest days of the winter have gone; since the shortest day (the 21st) the hours of daylight are once again beginning to lengthen, almost imperceptibly at first. In a sense, the light of Christ's birth banished the darkness away. This is what Christ does in any darkness—he pierces it with light, and he brings into it radiance and joy.

28 "In the world you will have suffering. But take heart! I have overcome the world." *John 16:33*

29 Each year we live we can look forward to the adventure of discovering more about God and his world; each year our relationship with the God of Love unfolds and deepens as we live in his company. Think about what you have discovered this year. Give thanks for any particular blessings that spring to mind.

30 Think over the events of the past year prayerfully. Commend to God each unsolved problem, each difficulty and sorrow. Trust him with your private fears, hopes, and dreams. Talk over your plans. Your life is bound up with his: he is the God who listens.

31 Offer to God all that you are now, as one year ends and another begins. Everything you offer he will accept, bless, and redeem. He is your God and you are his child, and you can walk together through the coming year, wherever it takes you!

Favorite Prayers

Use these pages to make a note of special prayers, readings, and intentions.